AUNTY ACID'S
GUIDE TO LIFE
CREATED BY GED BACKLAND

GIBBS SMITH
TO ENRICH AND INSPIRE HUMANKIND

HELLO THERE, FOLKS, WELCOME TO MY LITTLE BOOK ON L.I.F.E.

People who have nothing to do all day have pondered over the point of our existence since we were using sticks to make fire to heat up dinner (I still am as it freakin' happens, my microwave's been broken since the '90s)...

Well your favorite Acidic Aunty has been around the block a few times now and knows all there is to know about LIFE. Now that doesn't mean I'm a genius or anything, it just means I've made more mistakes than most people, in fact I've learned so much from my mistakes I'm thinking of making a few more just for the giggles.

So go ahead and delve inside for pages and pages of my wickedly witty and wise words on anything and everything from where to find that perfect gentleman (Warning: you may need to buy yourself a spaceship), to how to deal with all those freakin' idiots (let's just say it's about time some people started using glue instead of lipstick) and lots of other ballsy, bold, and brazen advice, straight from my cookie-munching lips to yours.

...AND REMEMBER

When life feels like a test you haven't studied for, Aunty Acid has the answers for you in the pages of this book.

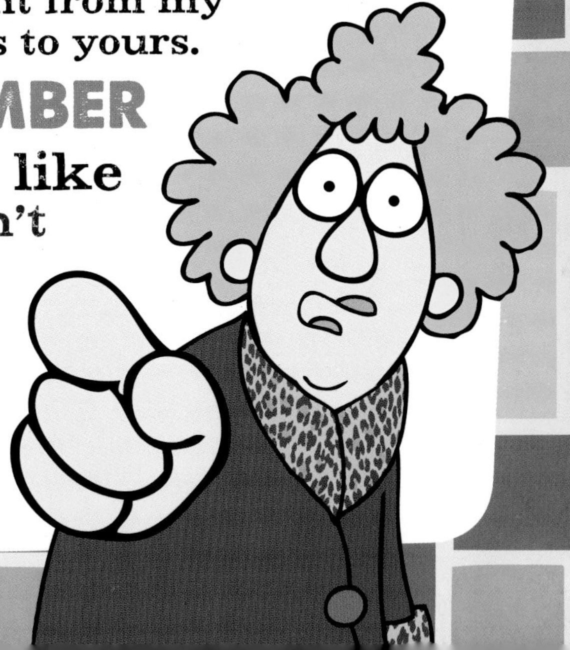

Unfortunately, my daydreams about **being skinny** are often cut short by the sounds of me chewing a cookie.

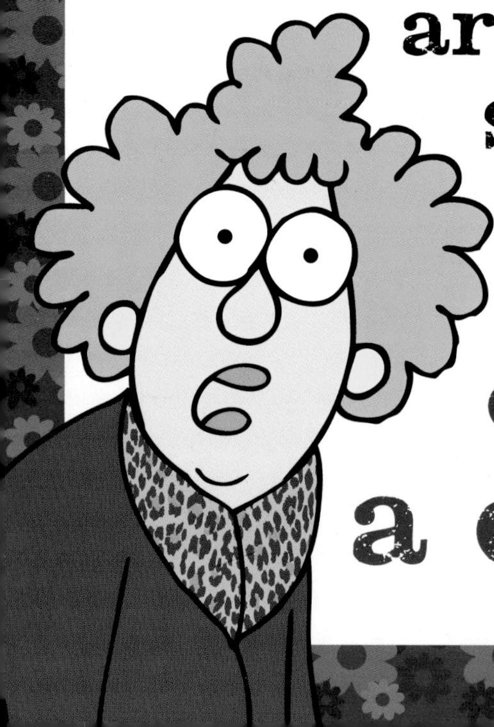

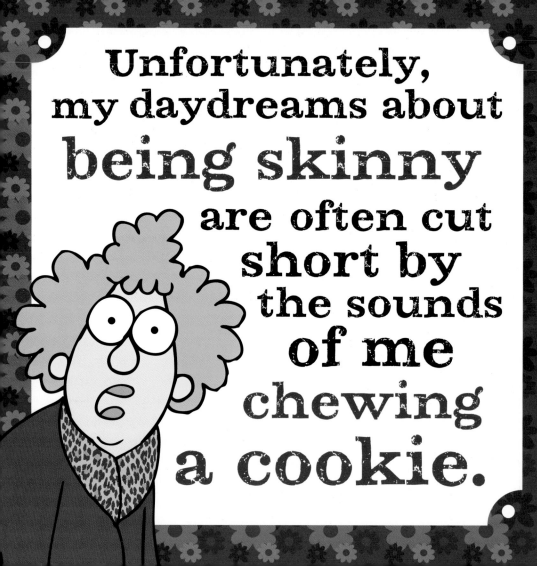

Wine
is
win
with
an e
on the
end.

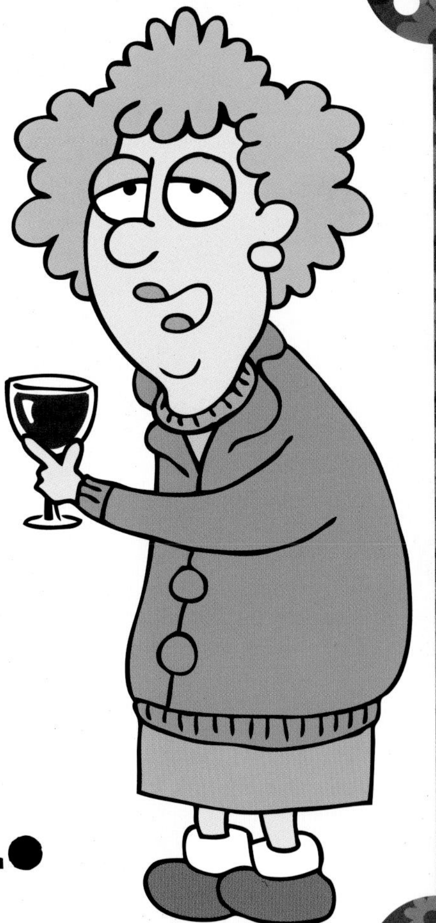

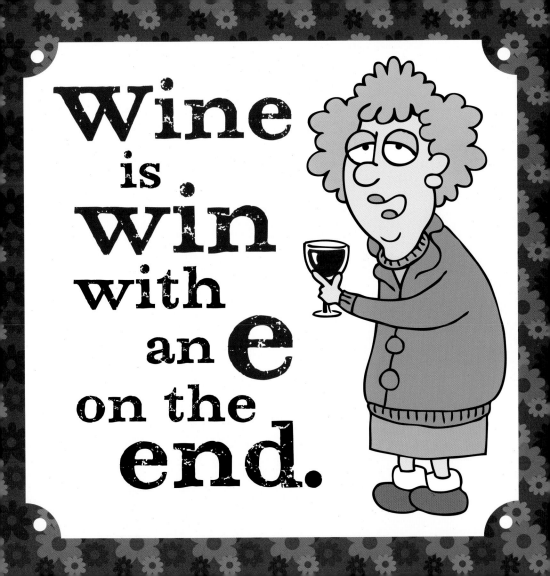

You can't always control who walks into your LIFE... but you can control which window you throw them out of.

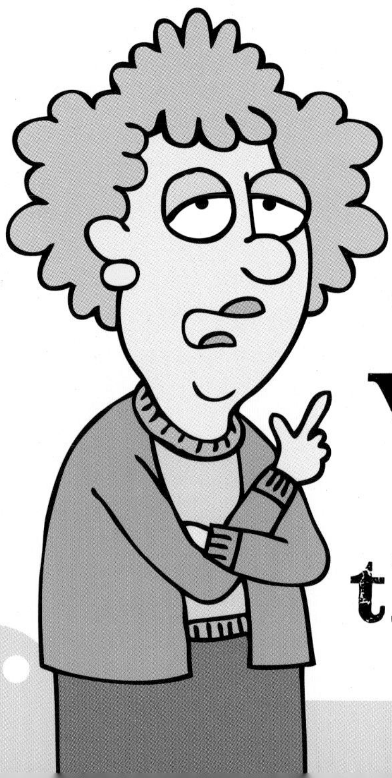

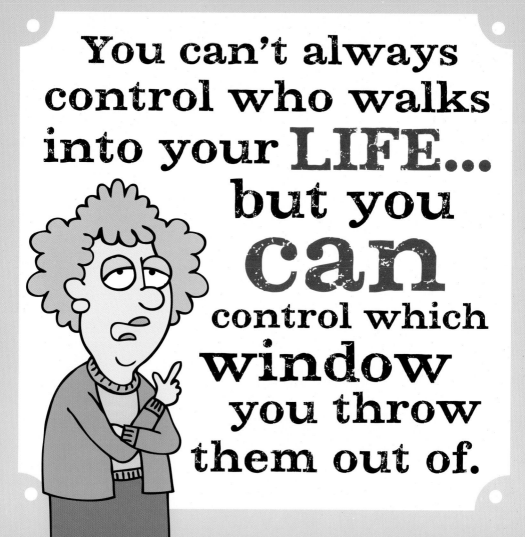

Life is

too short

to remove a USB safely.

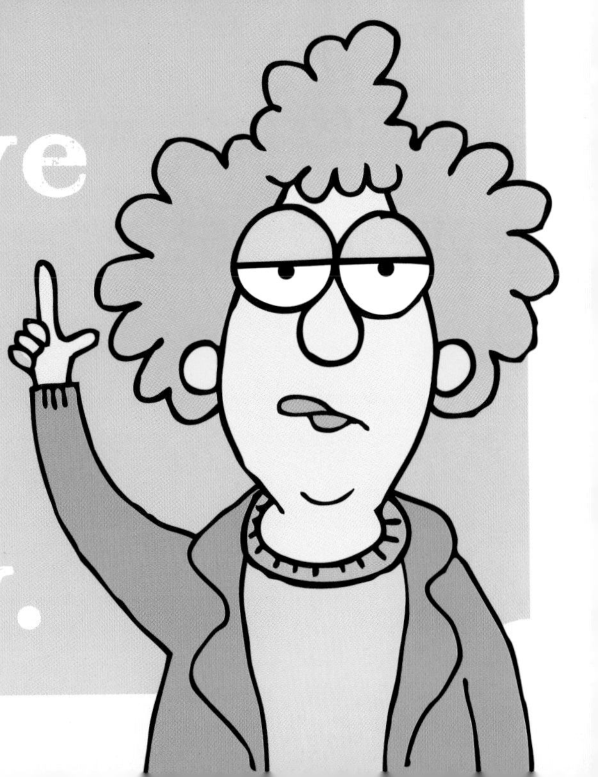

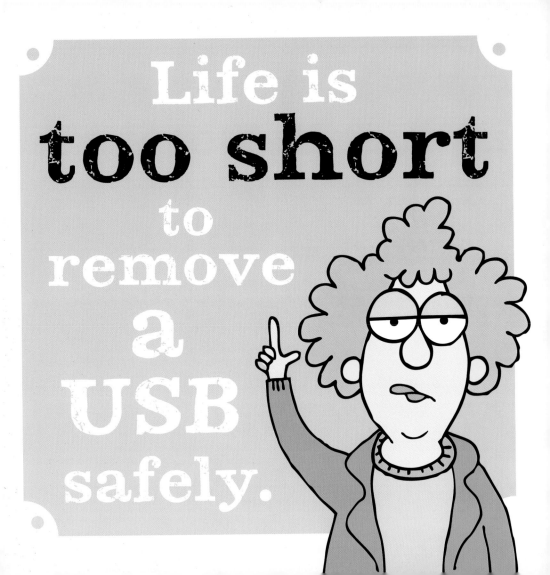

My second favorite chore is ironing. My first is hitting my head against a wall until I faint.

Is
A CASHEW
the
sound
of a
nut
sneezing?

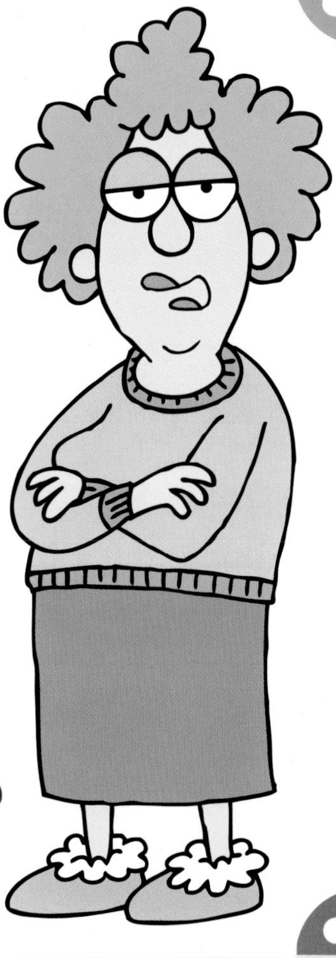

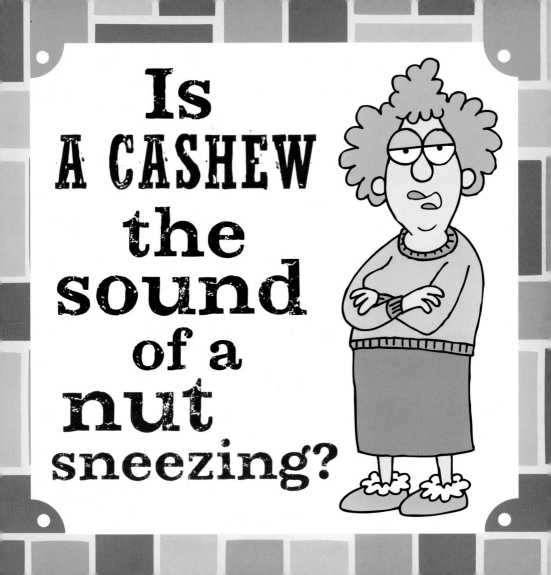

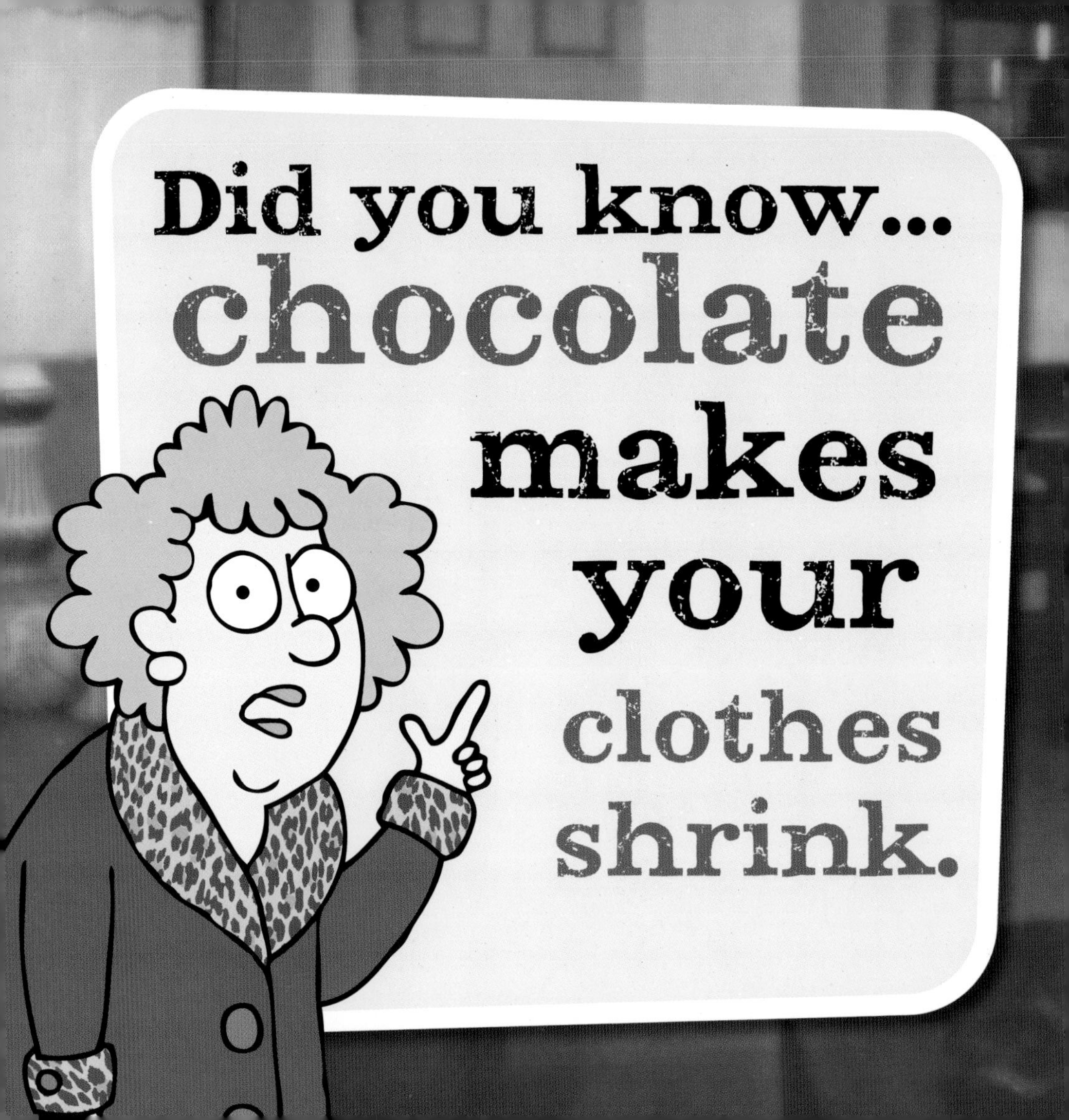
Did you know...
chocolate
makes
your
clothes
shrink.

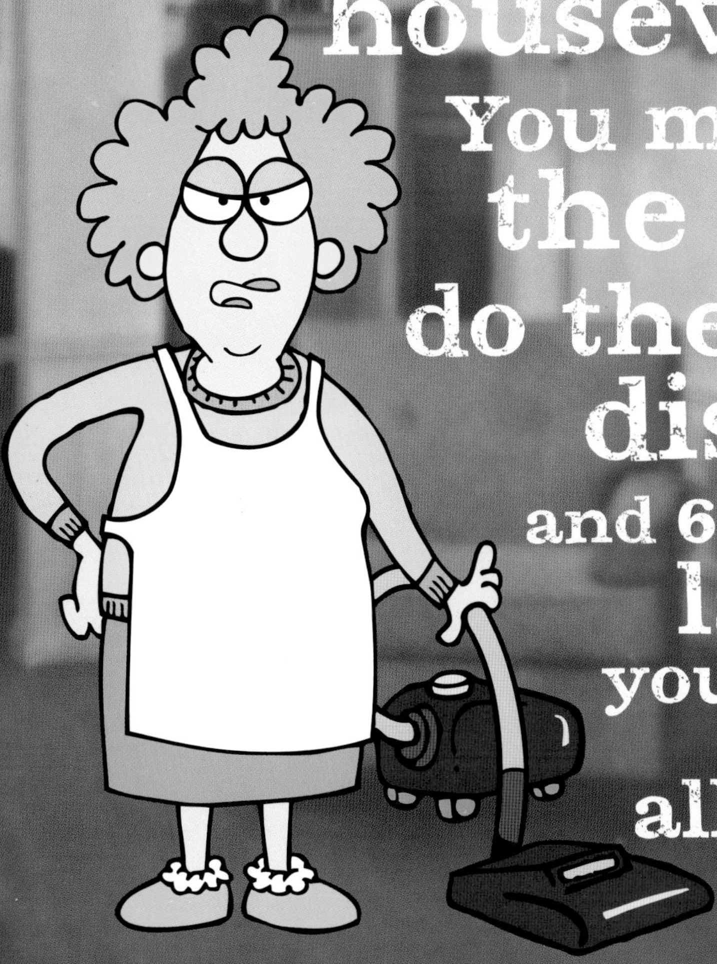

I hate housework.
You make the beds, do the dishes, and 6 months later you have to do it all again.

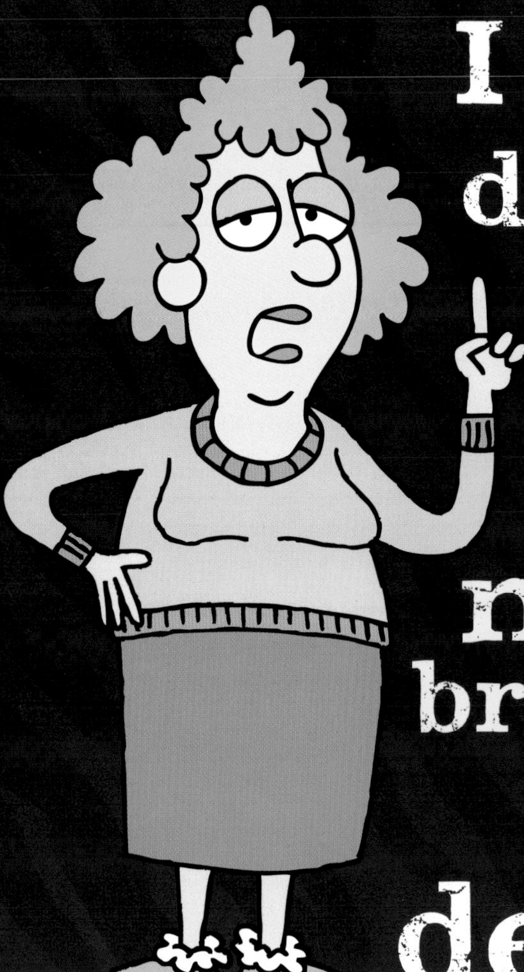

I just don't have **time** for the nervous breakdown that I deserve.

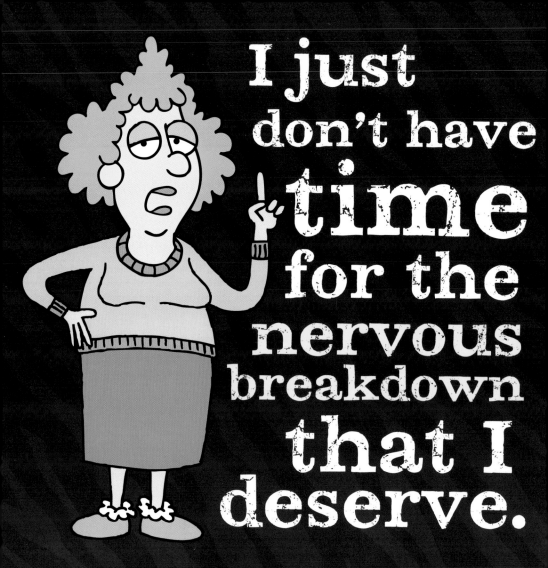

Go ahead,
seize the day
without me.
I'll just
have this
coffee
and catch
up with
you later.

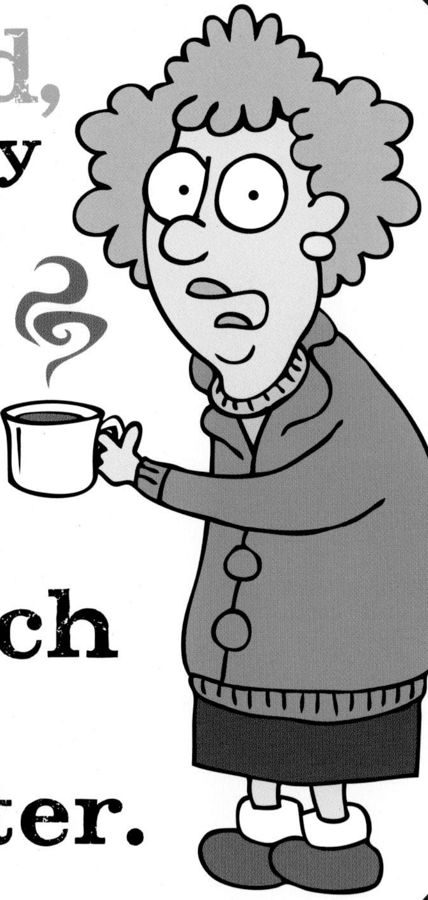

I have to stop saying, "How stupid can you be?" to my co-workers. They're starting to take it as a challenge.

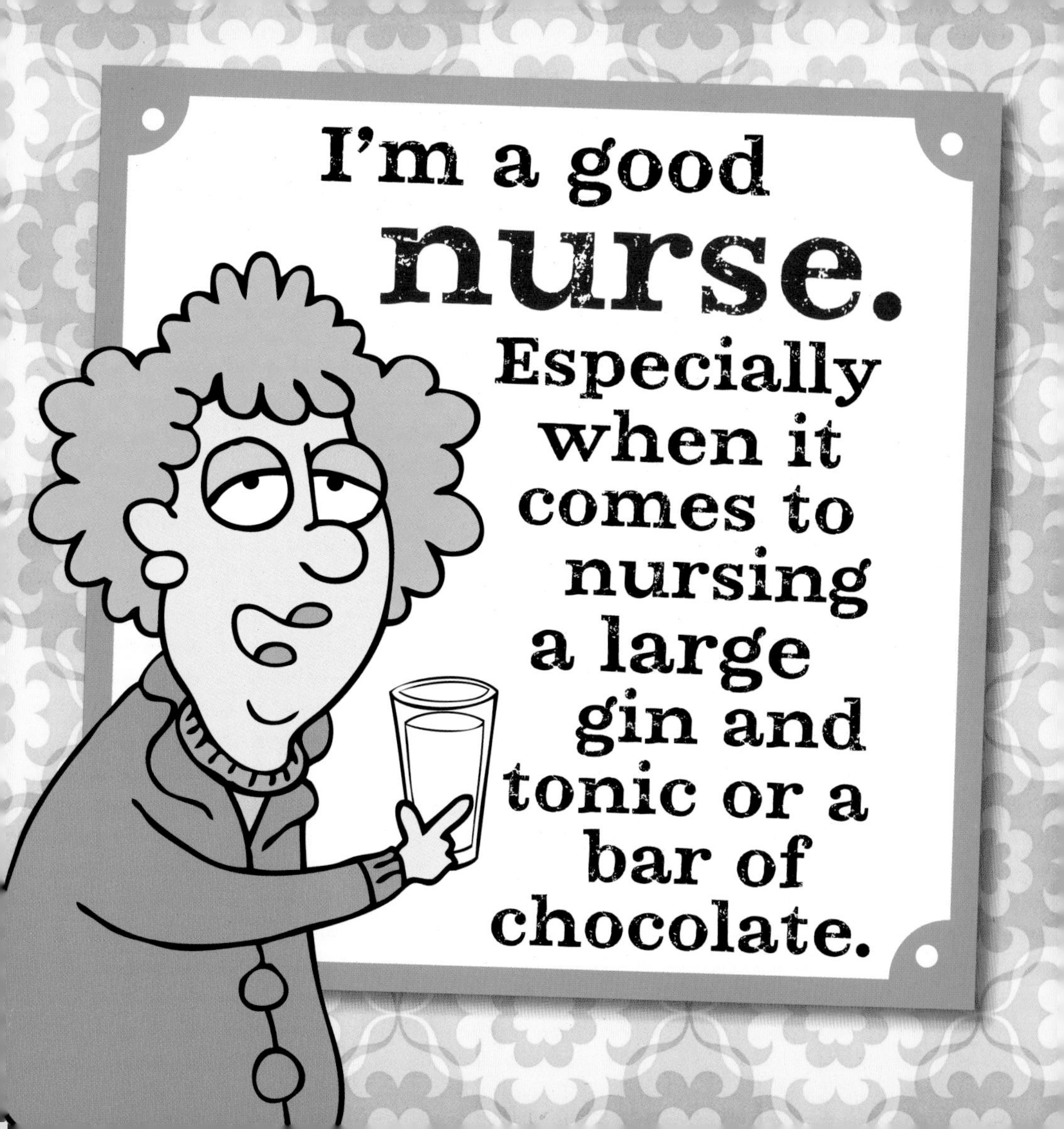
I'm a good
nurse.
Especially
when it
comes to
nursing
a large
gin and
tonic or a
bar of
chocolate.

Dear
Shaving Commercials,

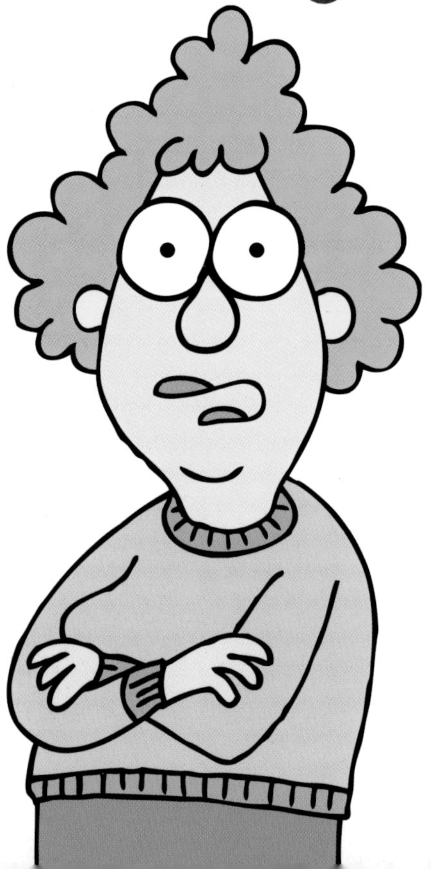

Stop shaving
hairless legs.
If you want
to impress
us women...
shave a
gorilla.

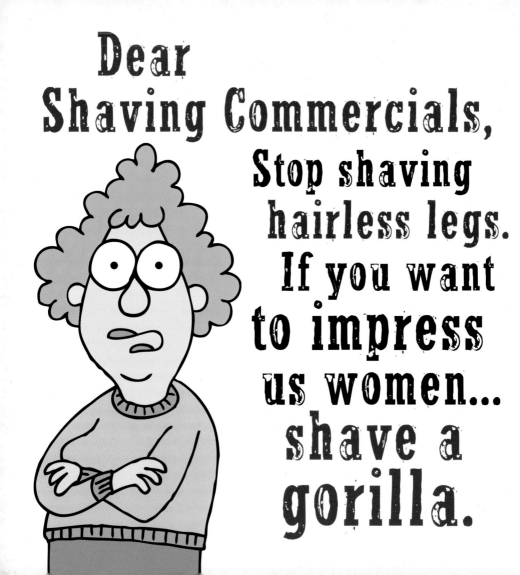

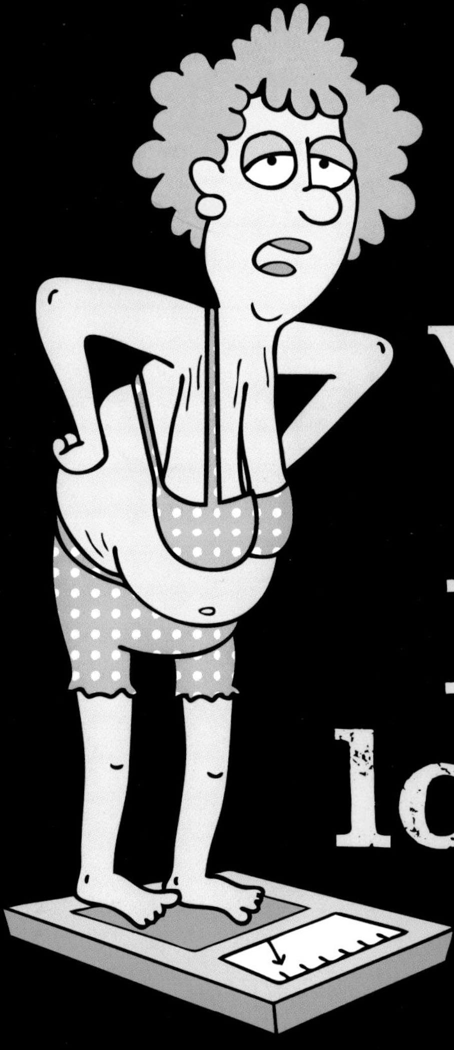

I'd lose weight...

...but I hate losing.

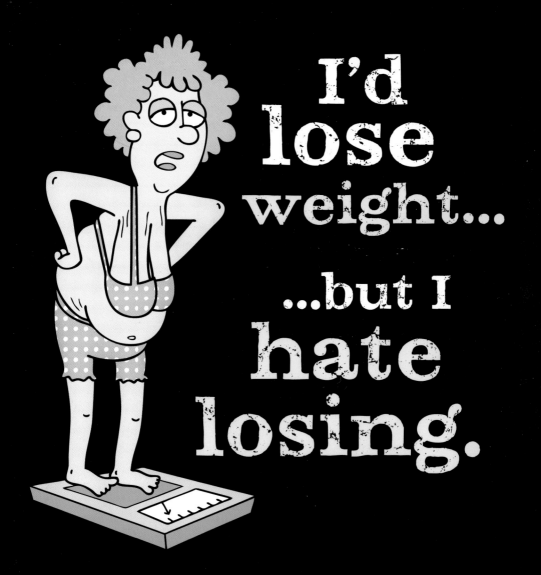

I eat cake

because
it's
somebody's
birthday
somewhere.

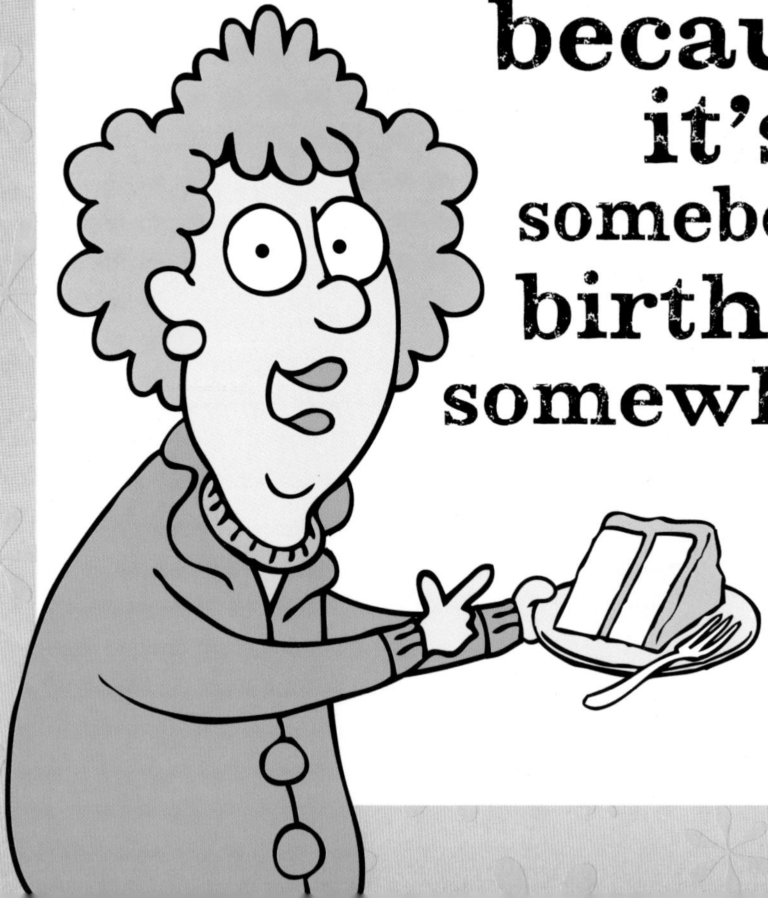

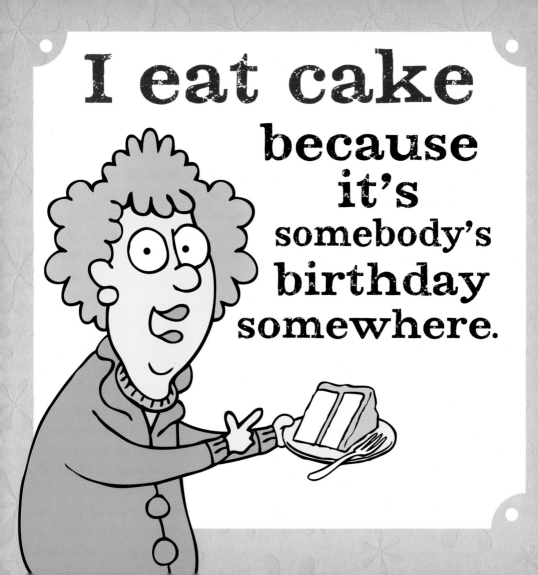

I try to take life one day at a time... but sometimes several days **attack** me all at **once.**

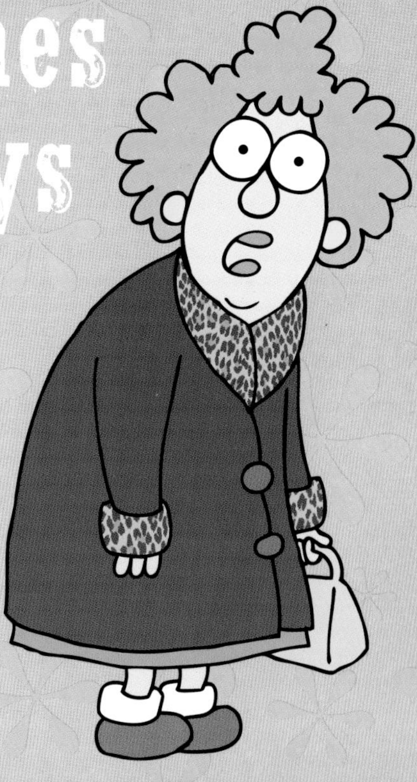

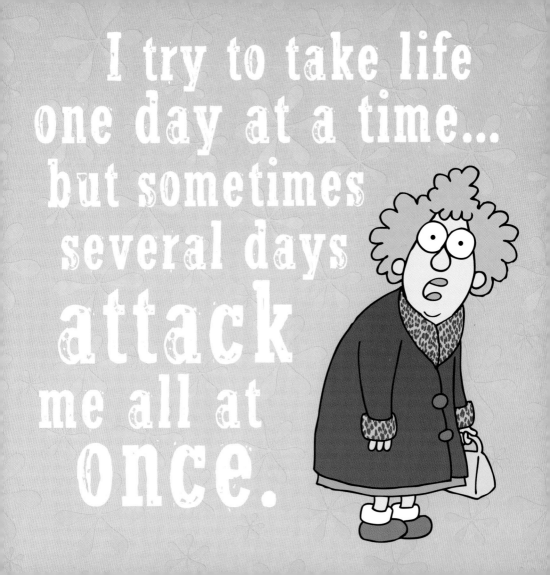

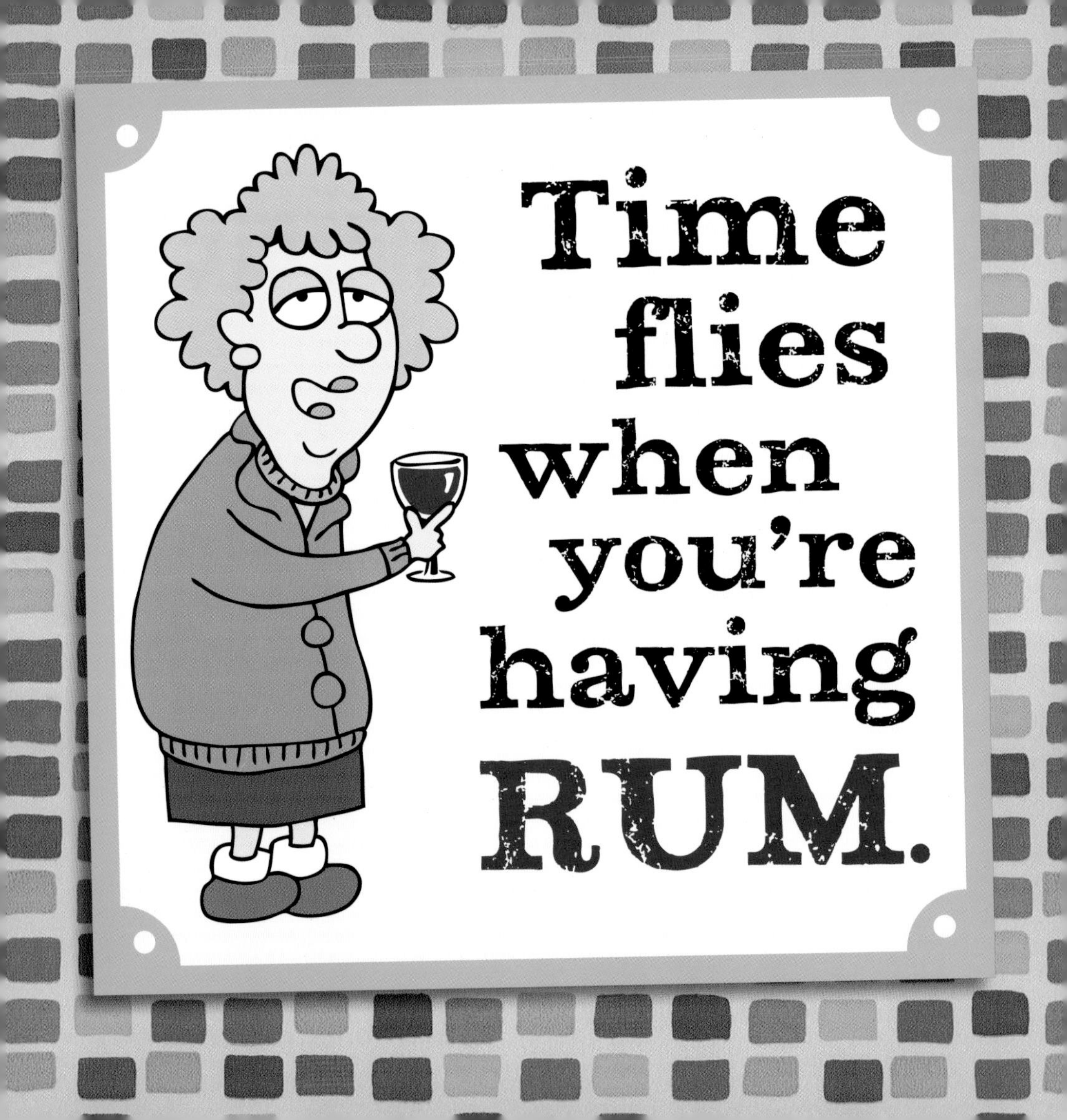
Time flies when you're having RUM.

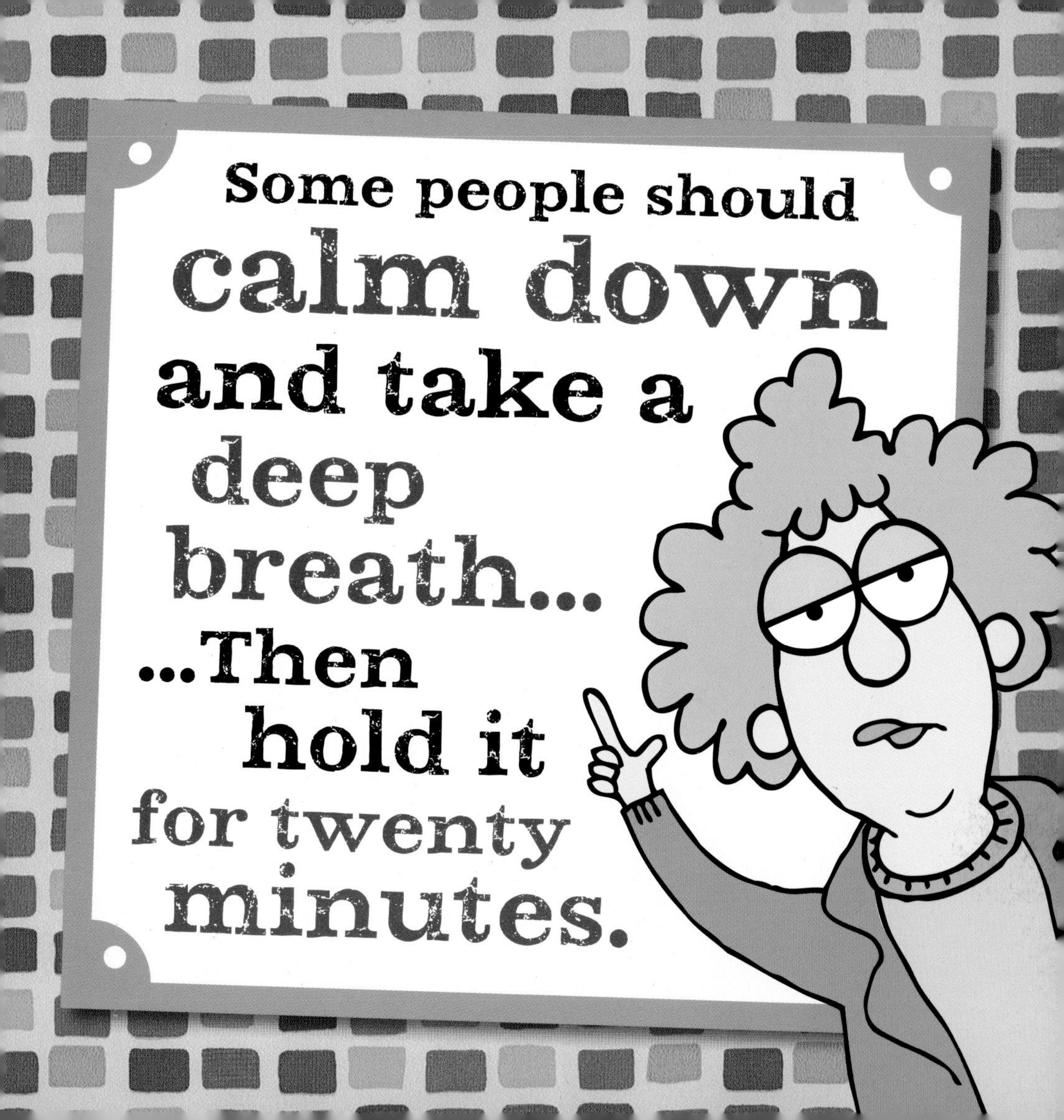
Some people should
calm down
and take a
deep
breath...
...Then
hold it
for twenty
minutes.

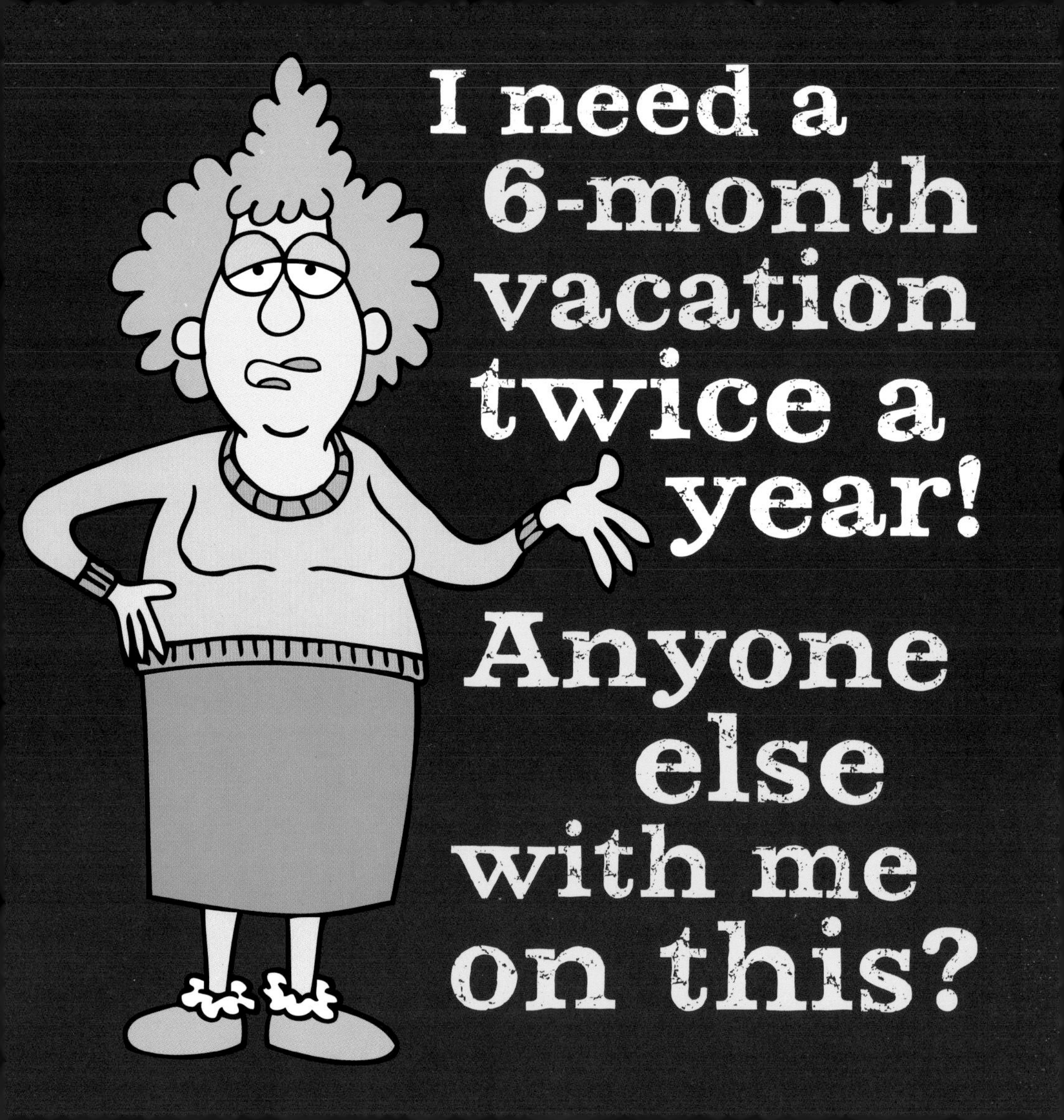
I need a 6-month vacation twice a year!
Anyone else with me on this?

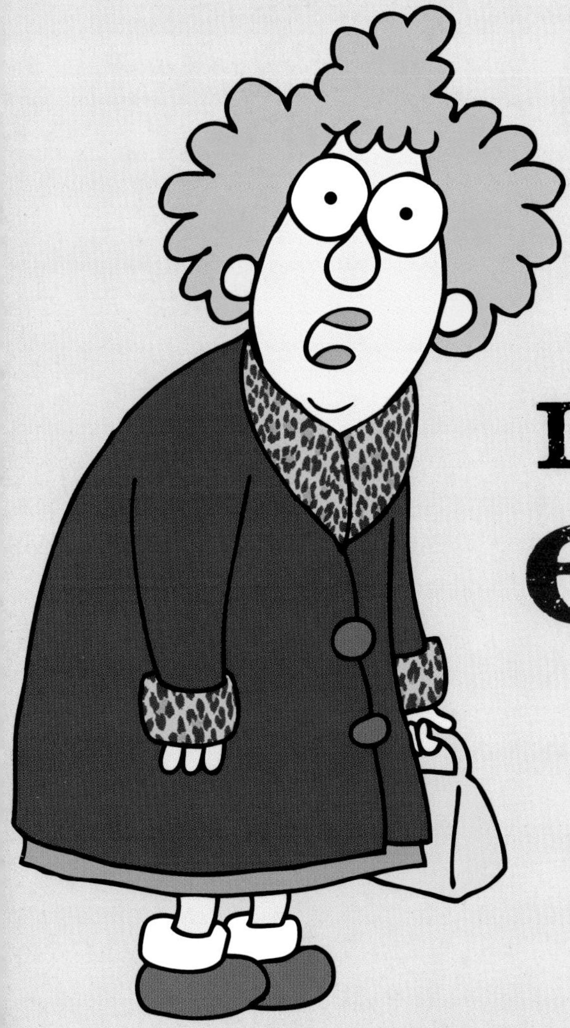

I'm not
fat.
I'm just
easy
to
see.

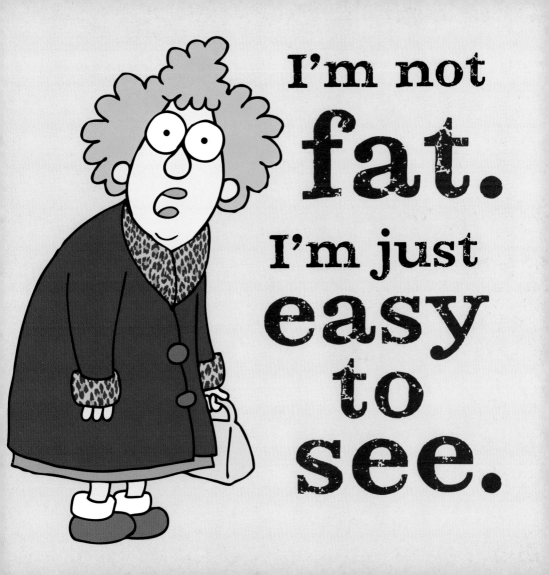

Sticks and stones may break my **bones...** but my foot up your **ass** is really going to **hurt.**

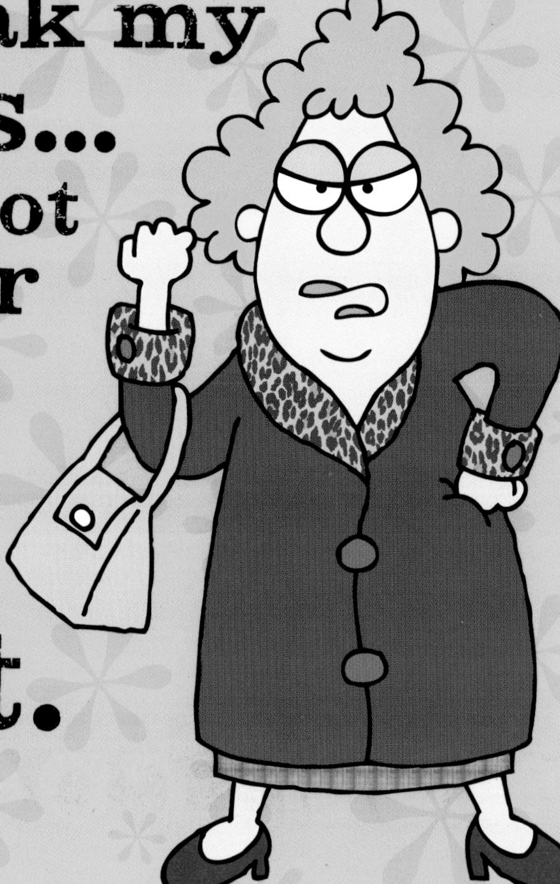

How to wash dishes:

1 - Place in hot soapy water.

2 - Tell yourself they need to soak.

3 - Go watch TV.

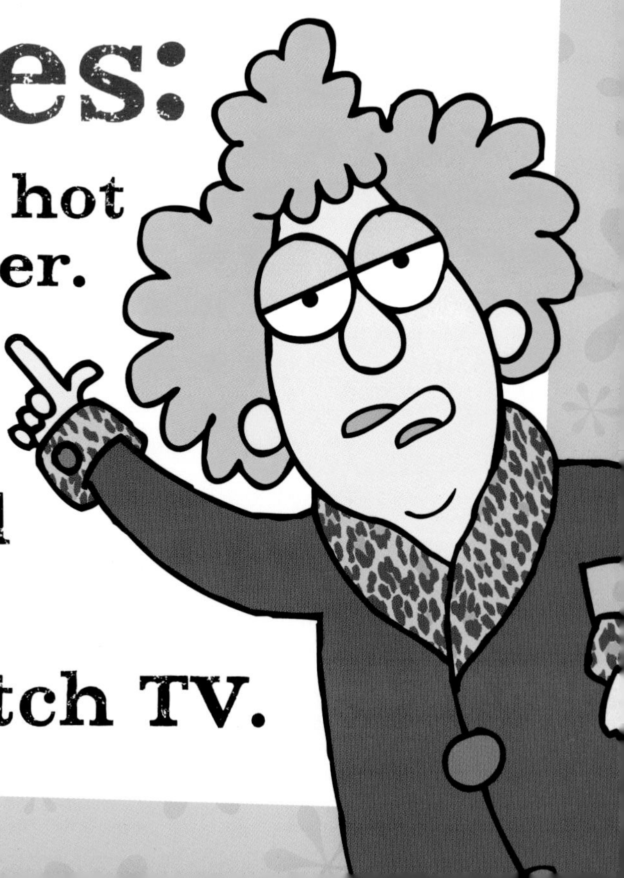

Therapy
HELPS
but
screaming
obscenities
is
faster
and
cheaper.

I DRINK COFFEE FOR YOUR protection.

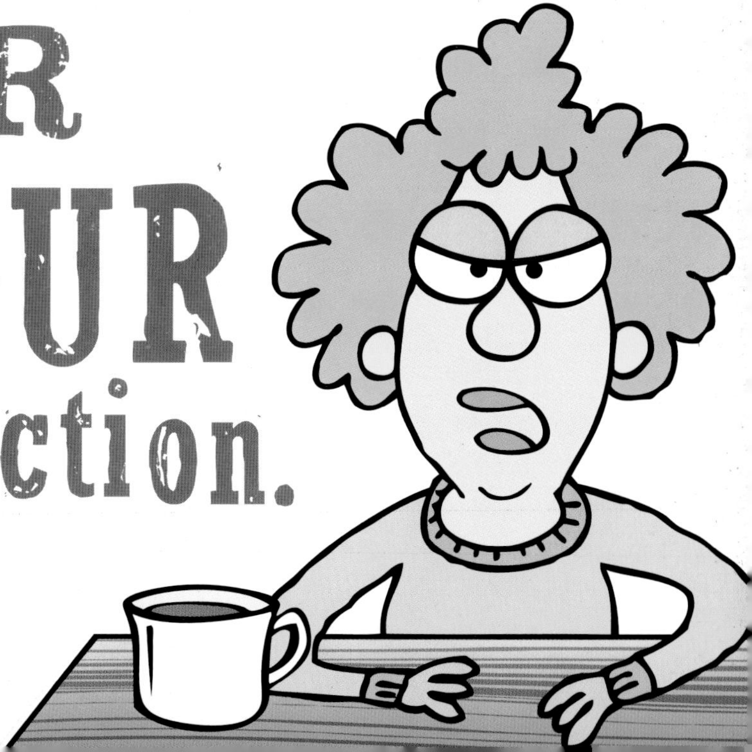

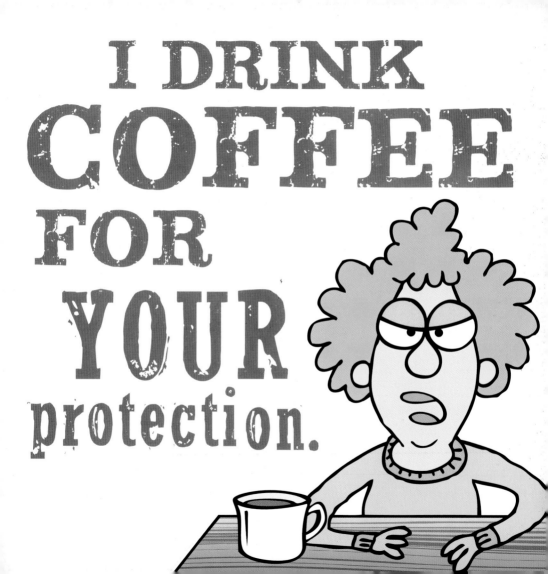

Sometimes I panic and think there's a **CRAZY** person in my house. Then I realize it's just me.

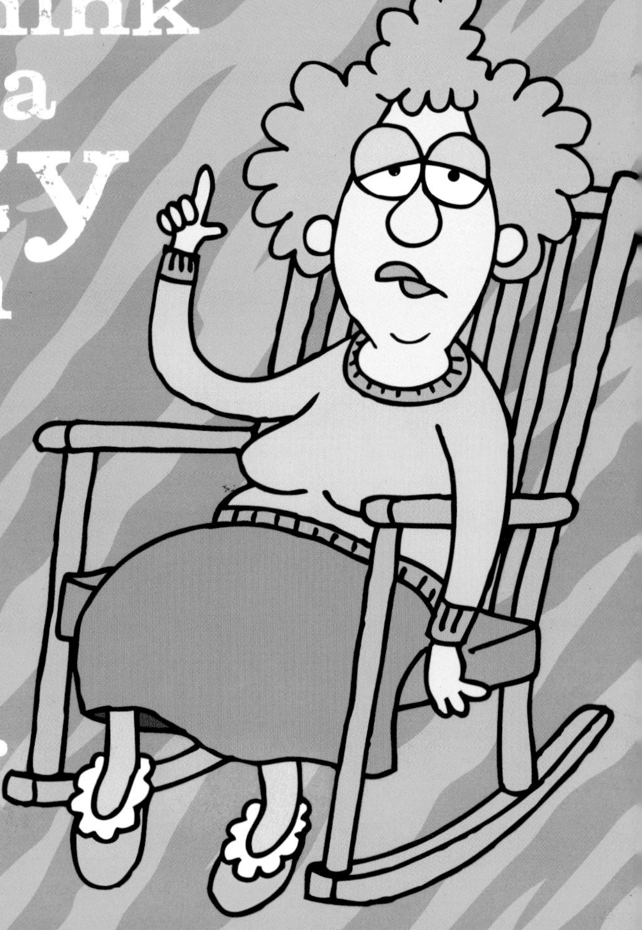

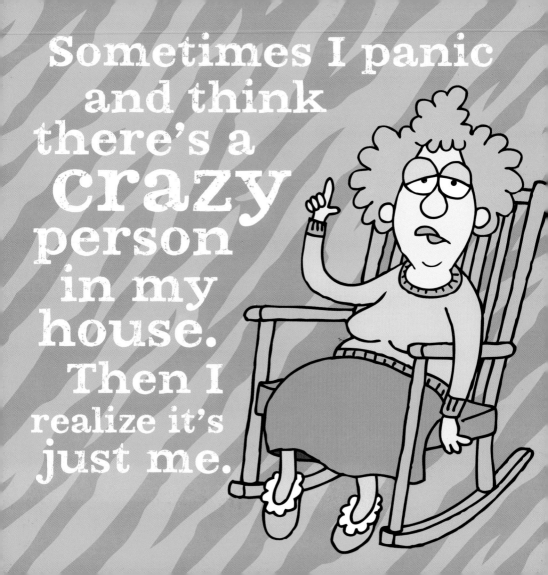

The best thing I make for dinner is reservations.

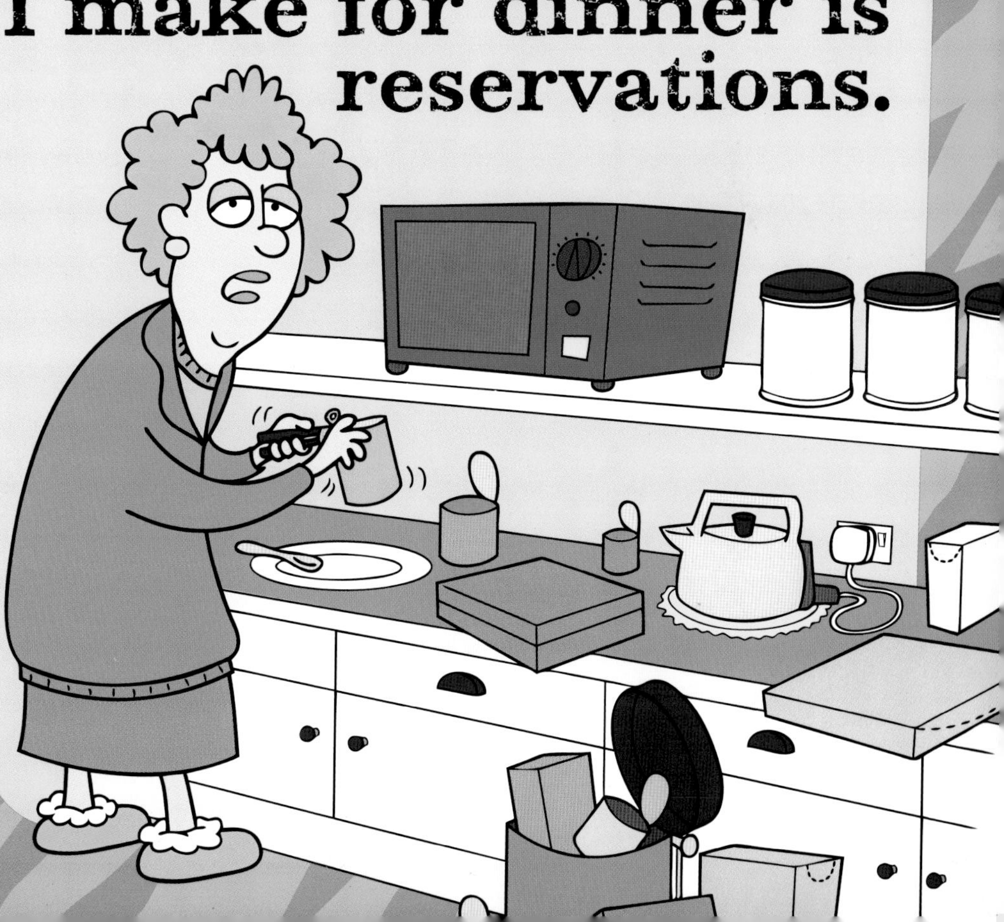

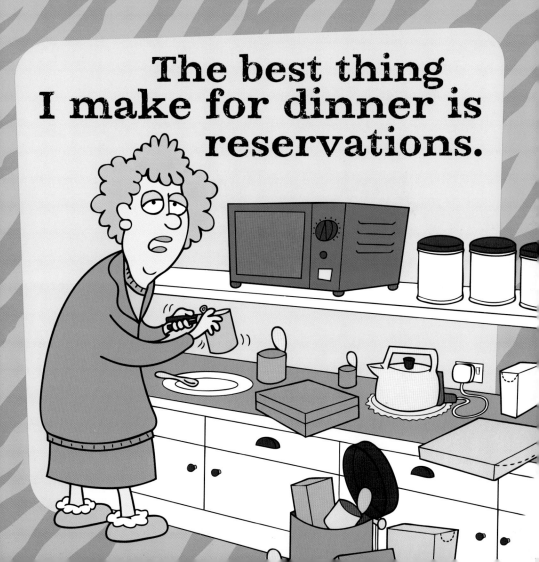

I have
PMS
and
GPS...
Which means
I'm a
BITCH
and I
WILL
FIND
YOU.

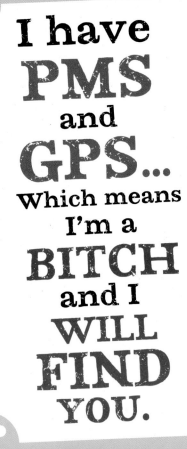

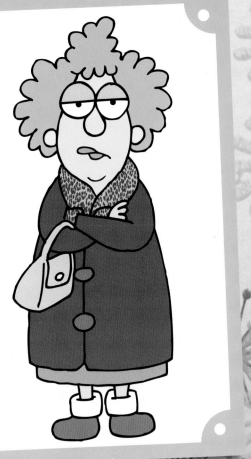

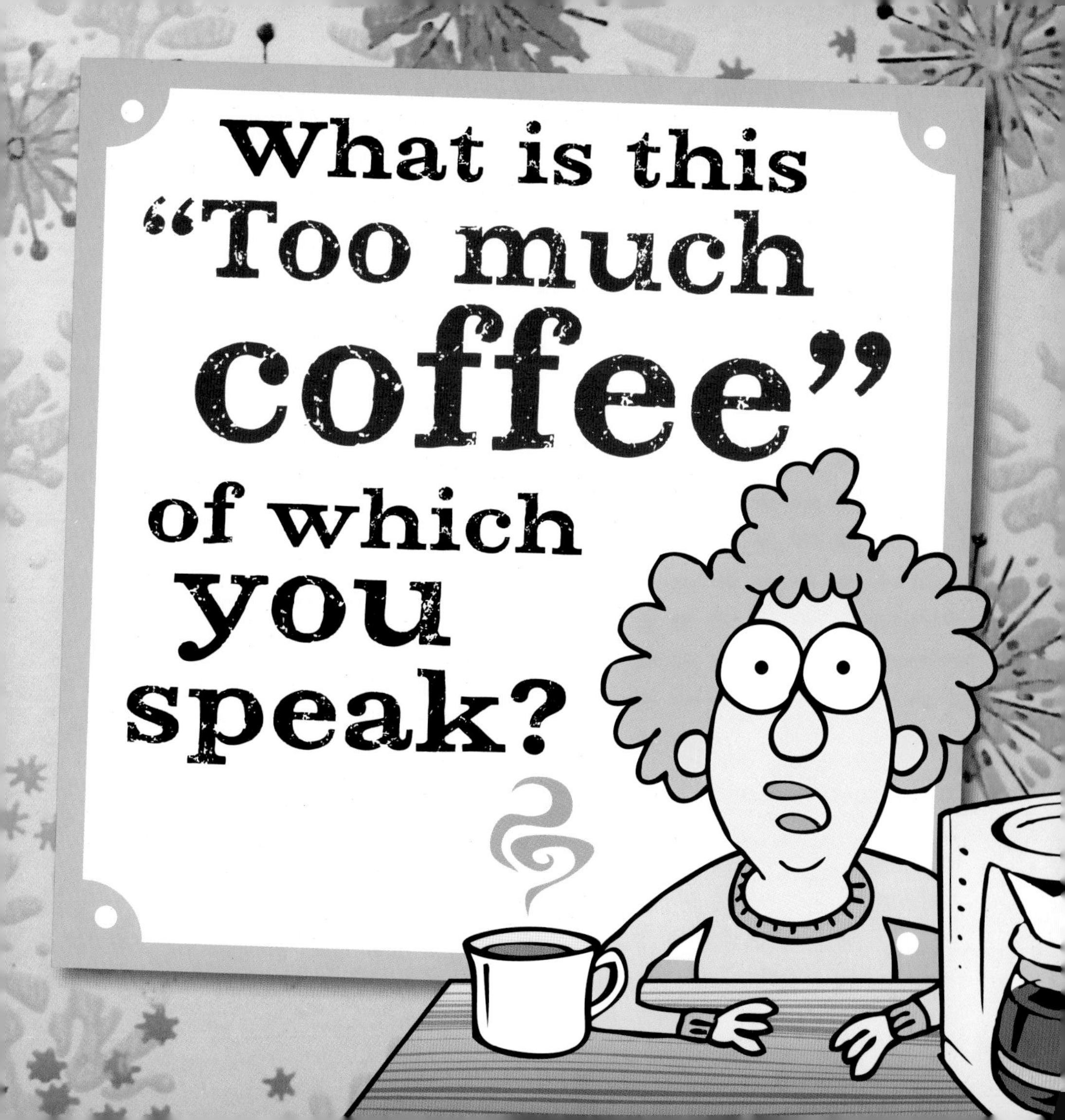
What is this
"Too much
coffee"
of which
you
speak?

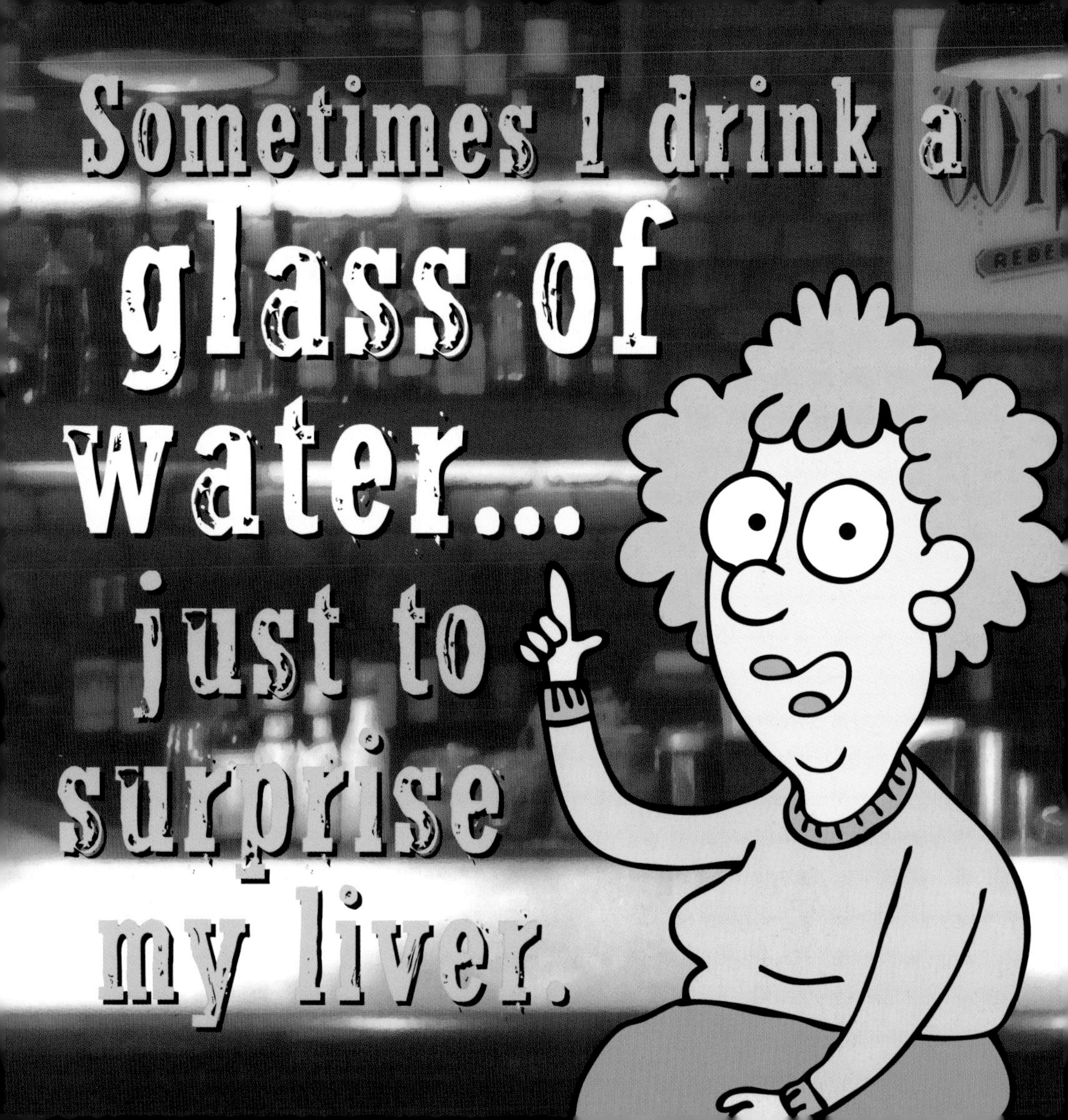
Sometimes I drink a glass of water... just to surprise my liver.

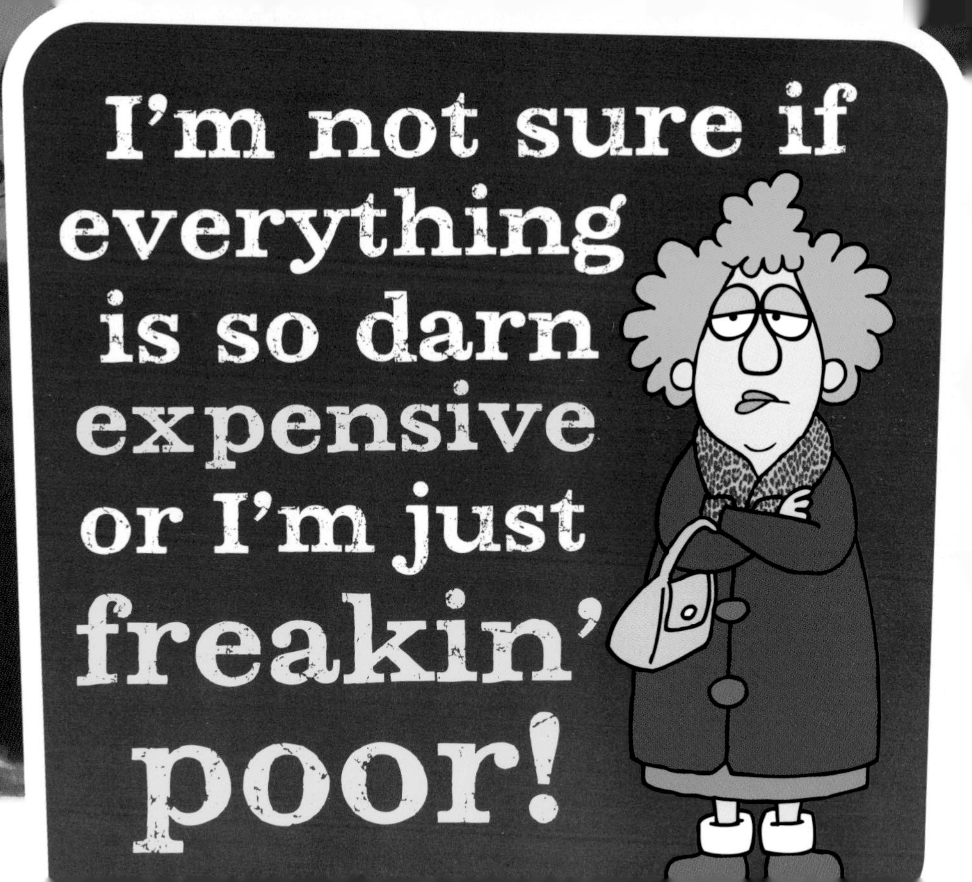
I'm not sure if everything is so darn expensive or I'm just freakin' poor!

PEOPLE WHO SAY NOTHING TASTES AS GOOD AS SKINNY FEELS HAVE OBVIOUSLY NEVER HAD BACON...

Hey, it's no secret that I always start my diet on the same day... Tomorrow!

Unfortunately, more often than not, my daydreams of being skinny are interrupted by the sound of me eating cake (Hell, it's always someone's birthday somewhere, right?) So read on for some of my best ditties on cooking, the perils of dieting, the magic of caffeine and the wonders of wine...

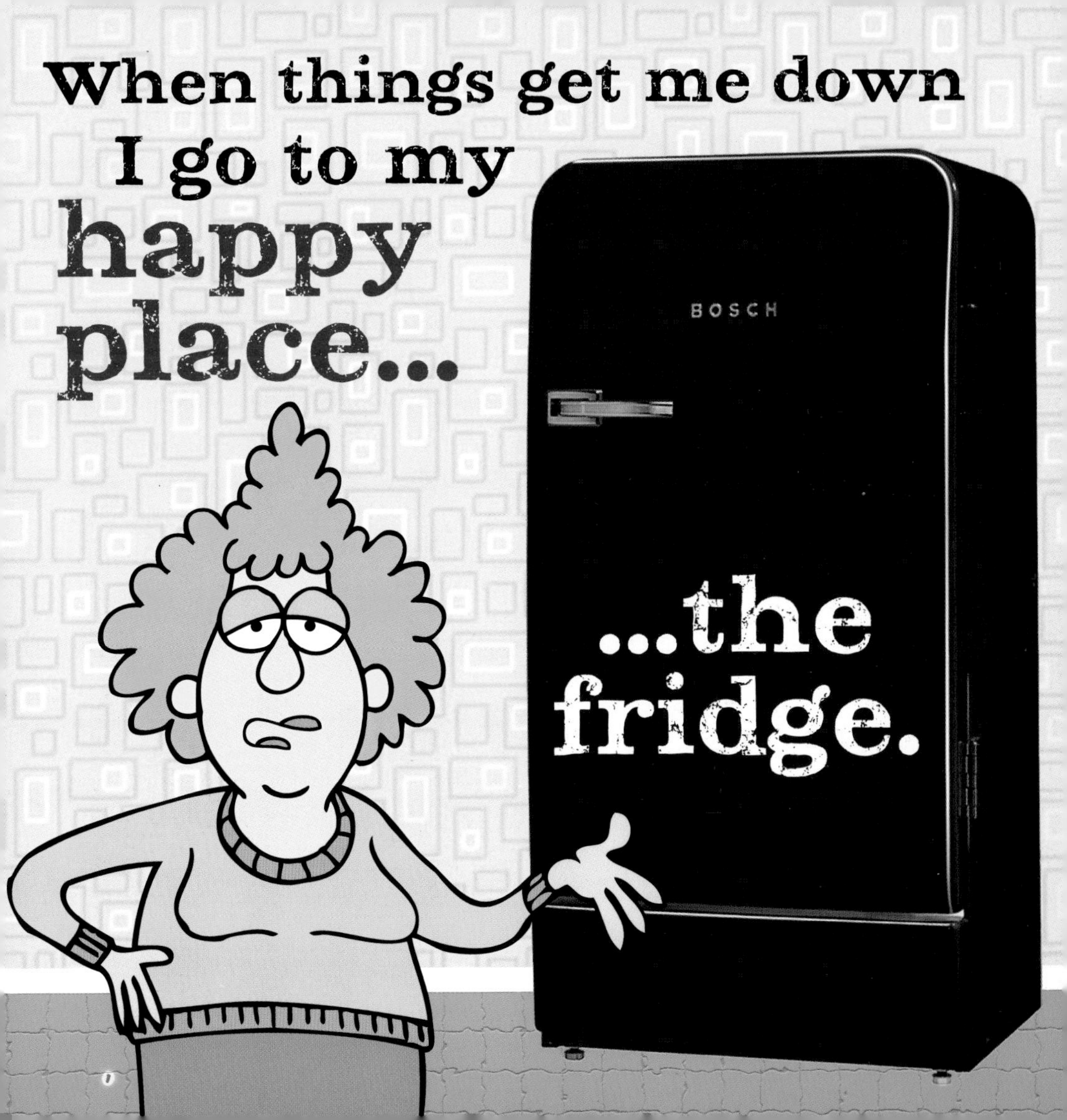
When things get me down
I go to my
happy
place...
BOSCH
...the
fridge.

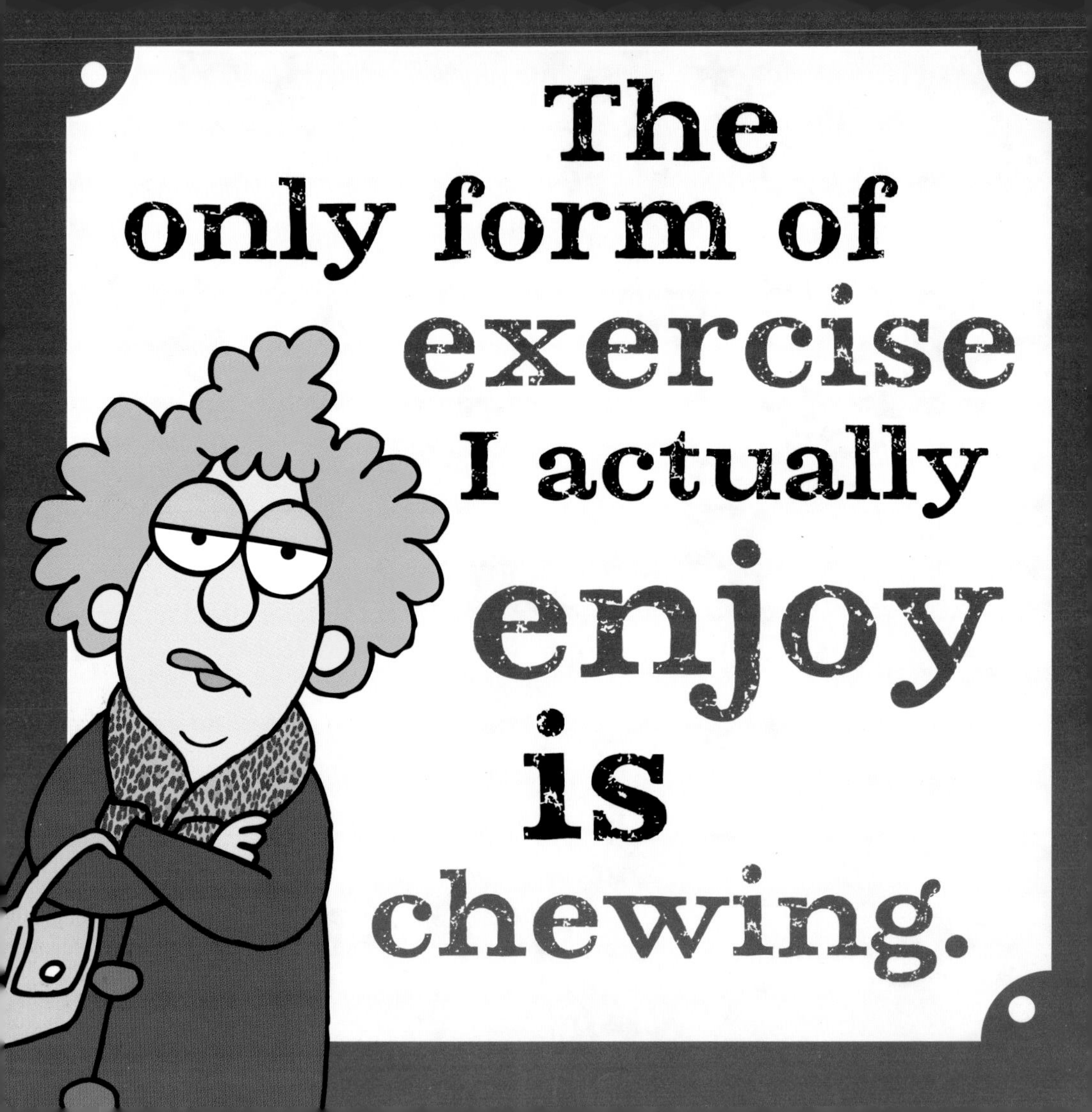
The only form of exercise I actually enjoy is chewing.

I've taken up photography because it's the only hobby where I can shoot people and cut their heads off without going to jail.

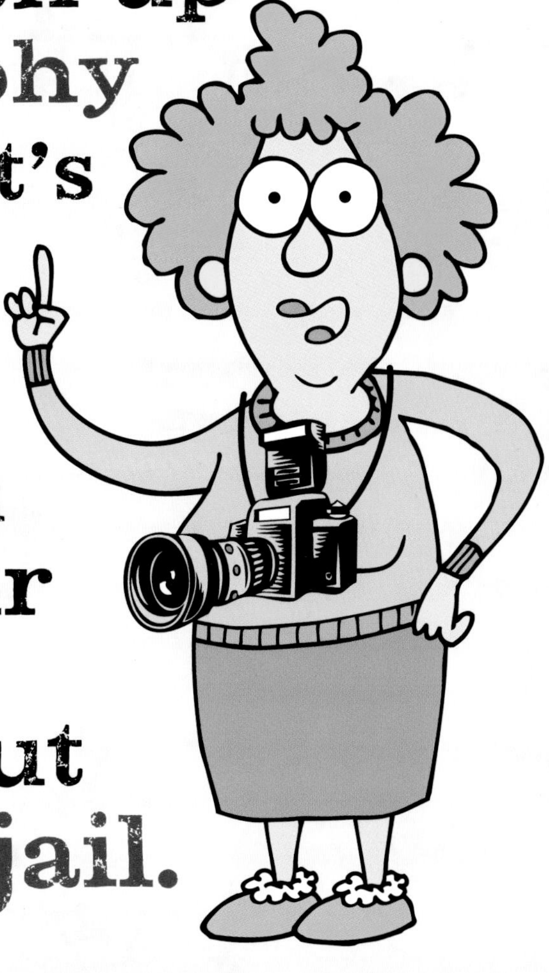

Everything happens for a reason

and sometimes the reason is that you're freakin' stupid and made a bad decision.

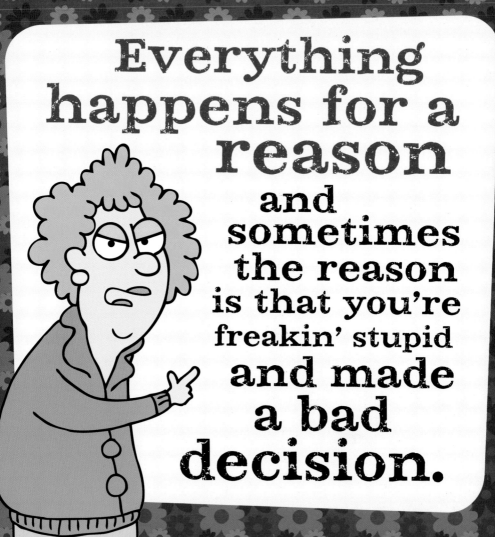

I think I'm emotionally constipated.

I haven't given a crap all week.

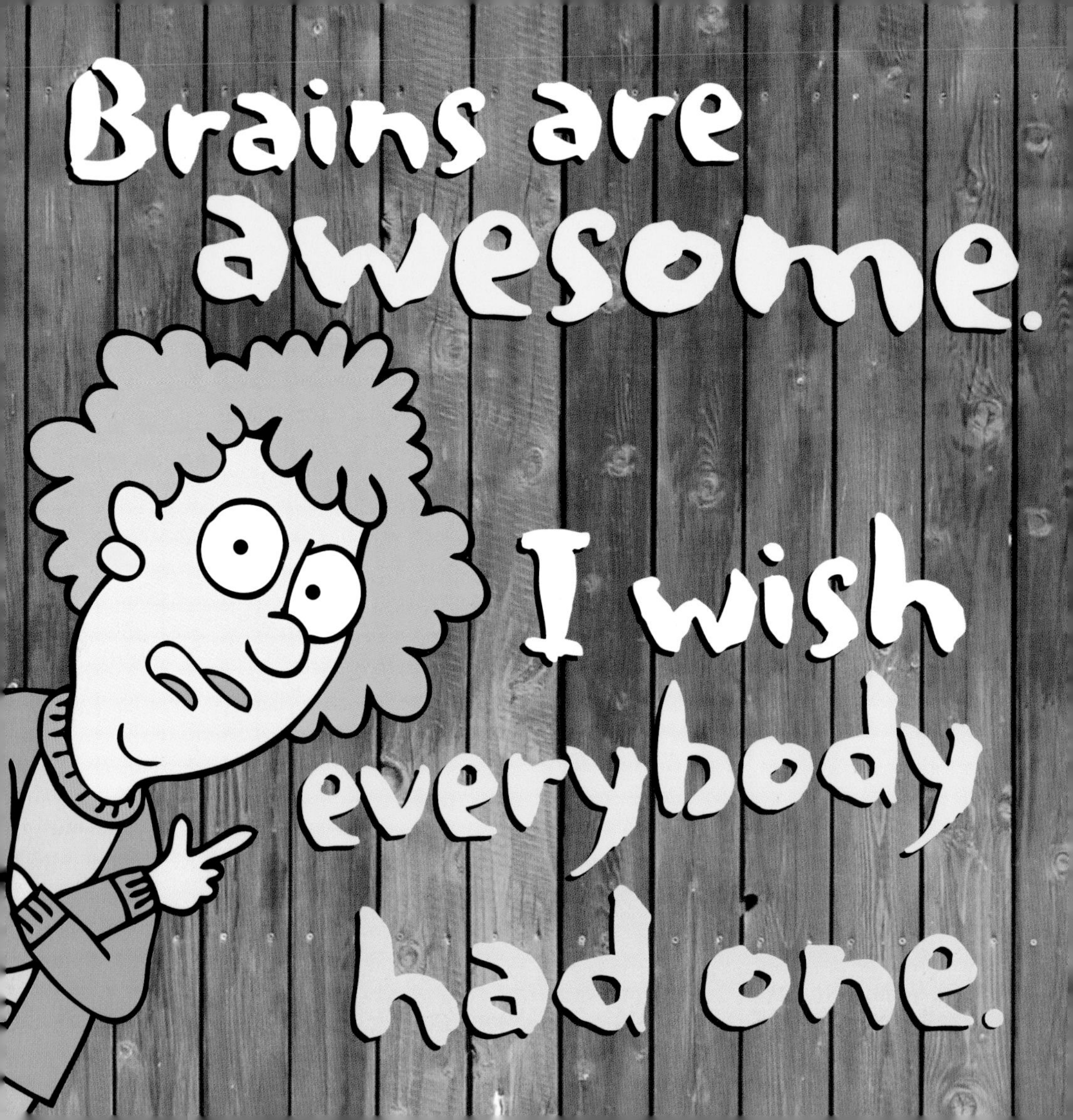
Brains are awesome.
I wish everybody had one.

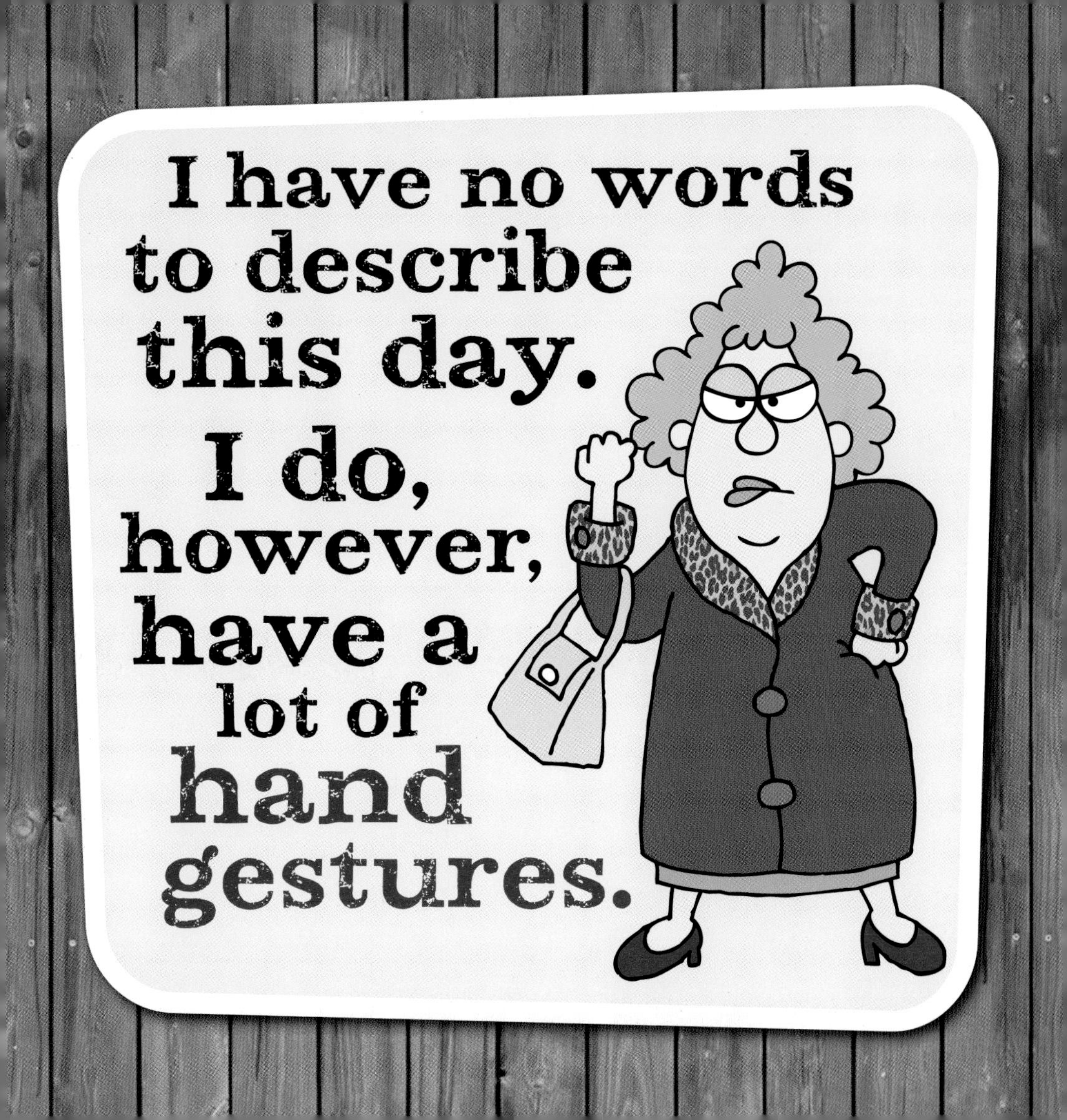
I have no words
to describe
this day.
I do,
however,
have a
lot of
hand
gestures.

Some people speak so much

crap

it's difficult to know whether to offer them toilet paper or a breath

mint.

Do I have any weight-loss mantras?

Fat chants!

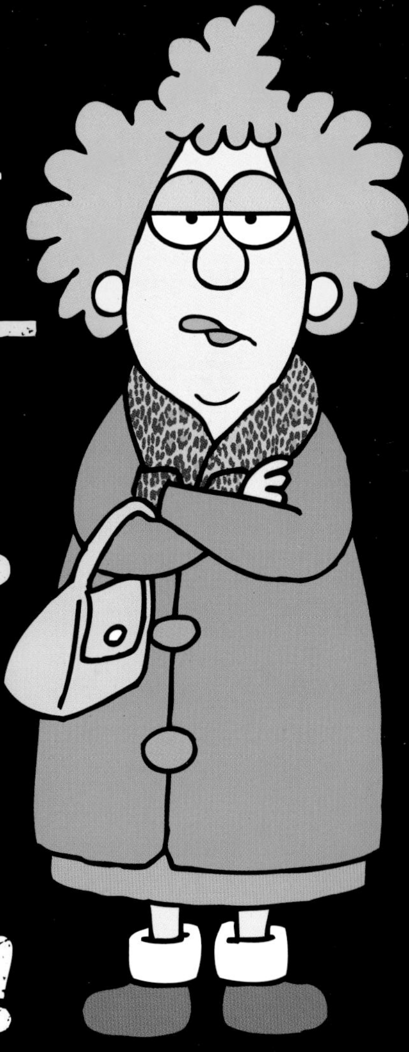

A good day is when the crap hits the fan and I have time to duck.

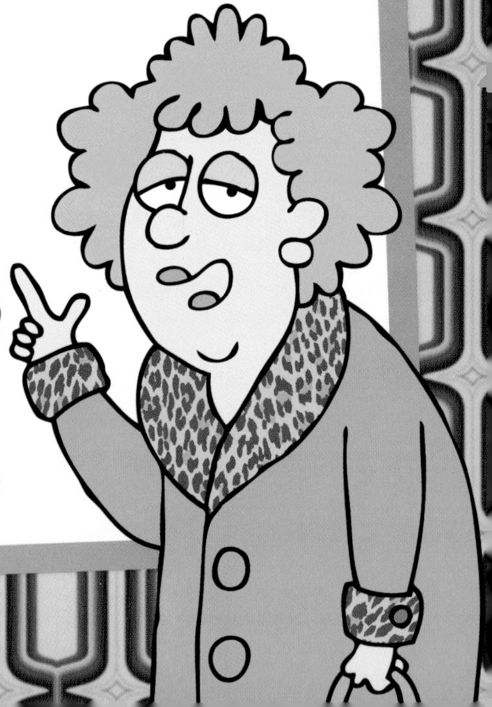

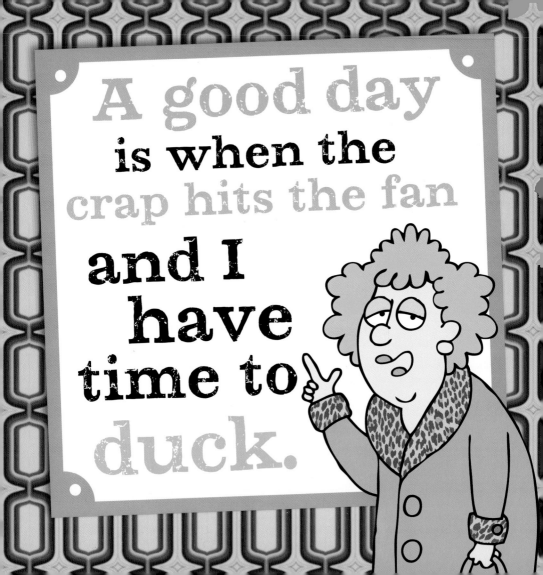

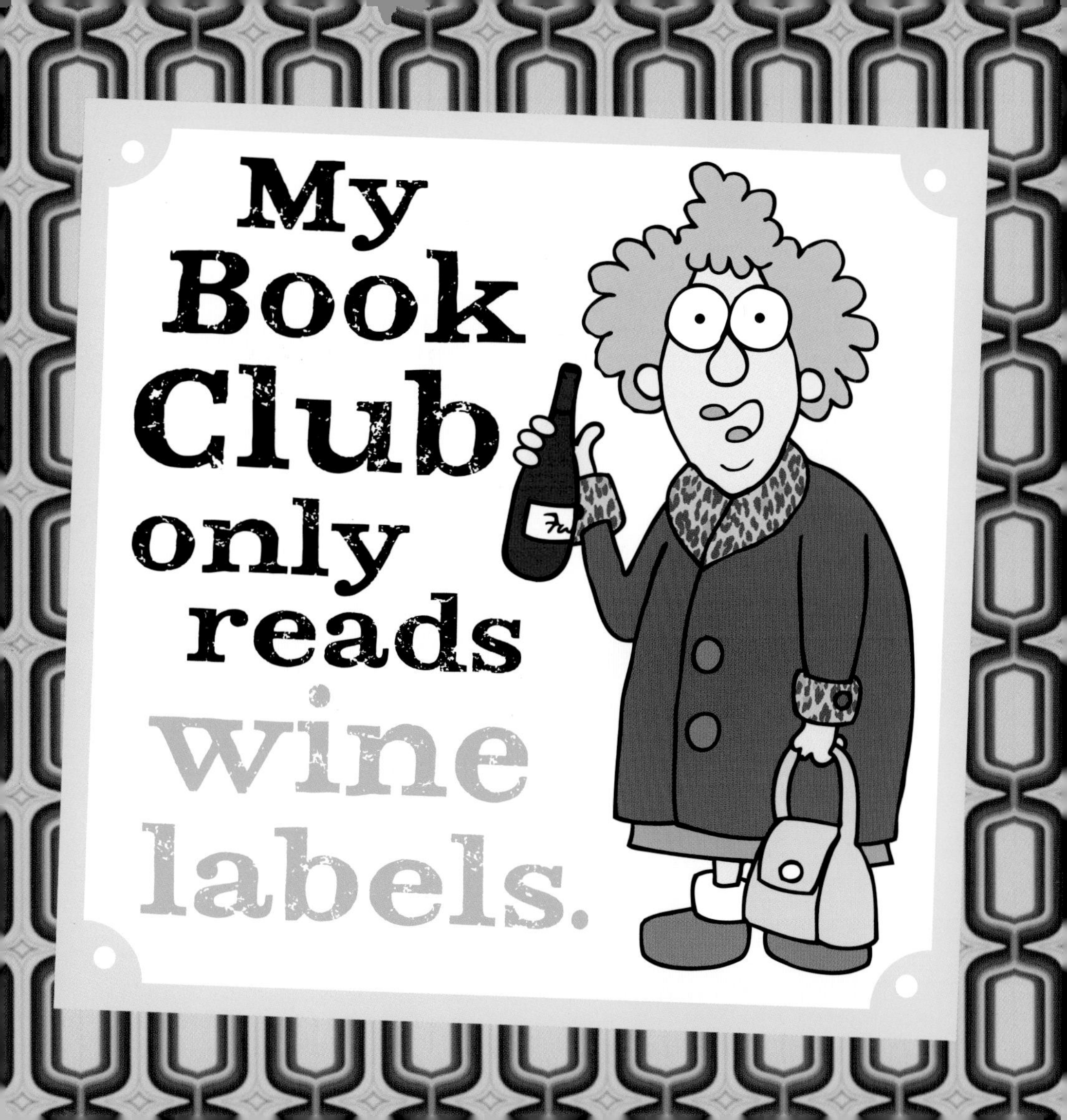
My
Book
Club
only
reads
wine
labels.

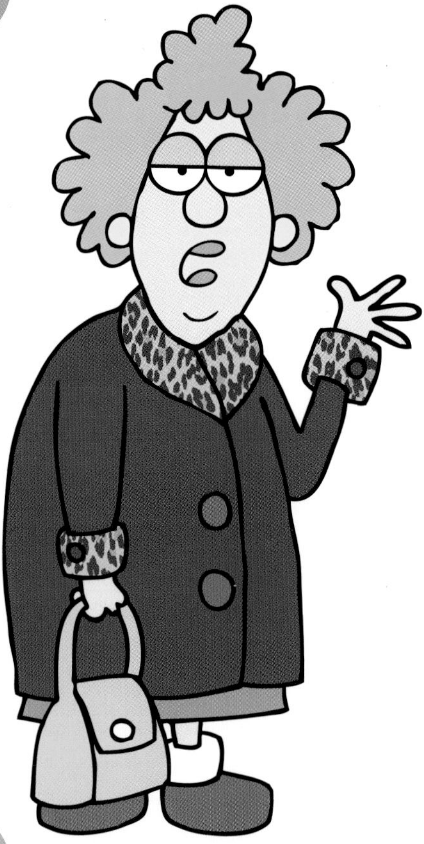

Pets. Like having kids without the stretch marks.

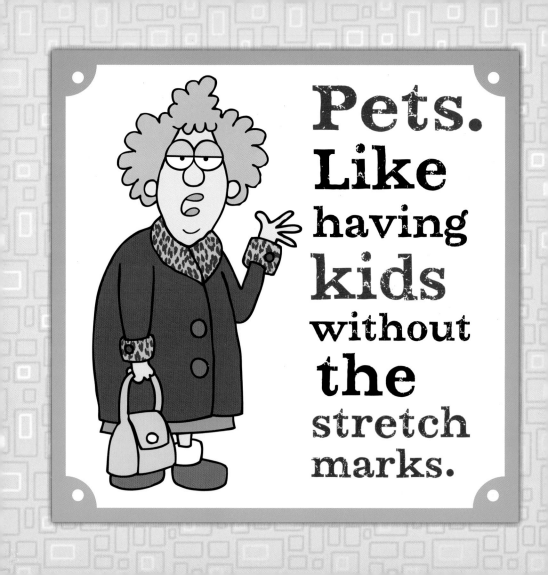

I wouldn't have to manage my **anger** if people **would** manage their freakin' stupidity.

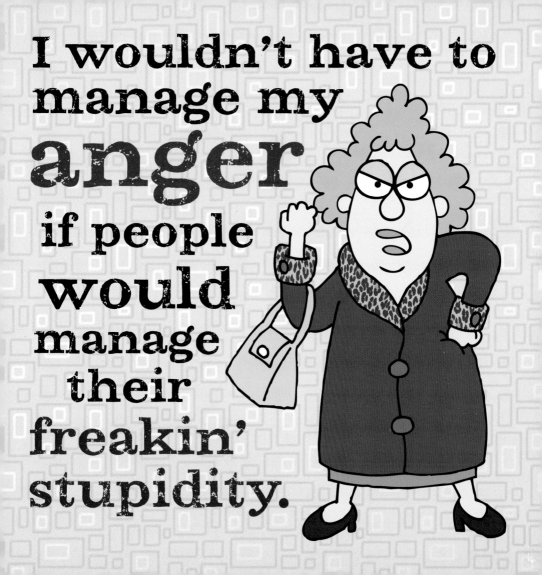

Be happy

in front of people you don't like.

It kills them.

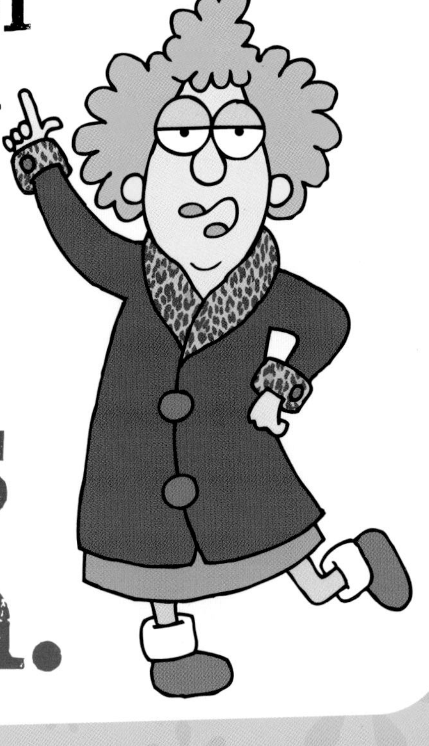

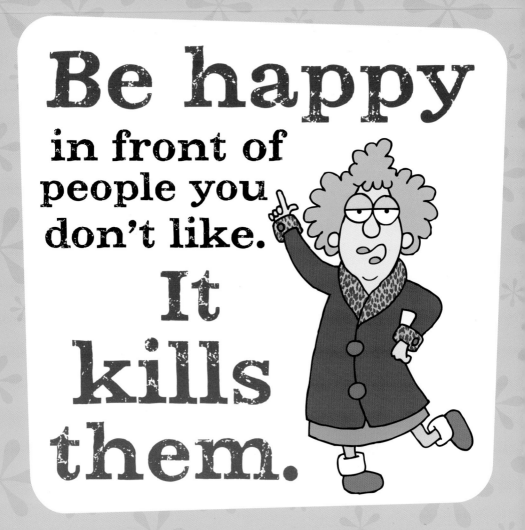

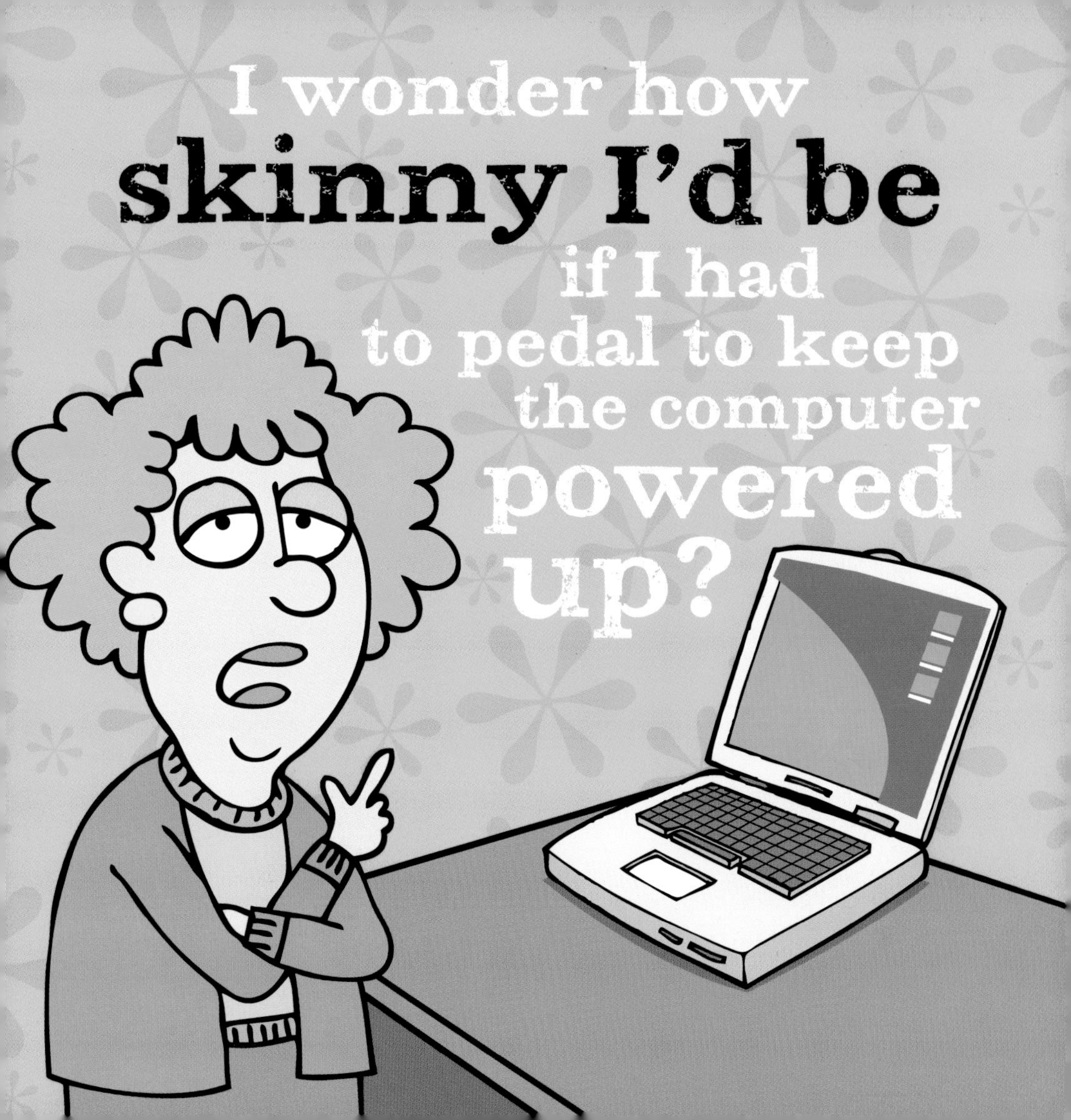
I wonder how
skinny I'd be
if I had
to pedal to keep
the computer
powered
up?

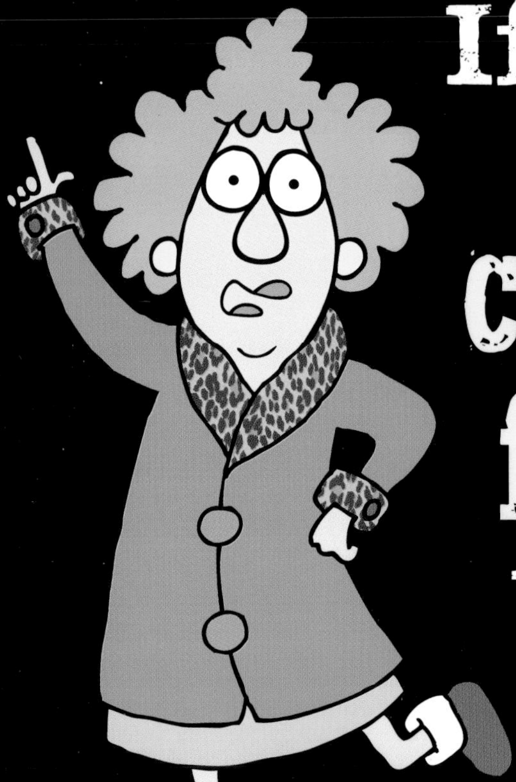

If you have crazy friends, then you have everything.

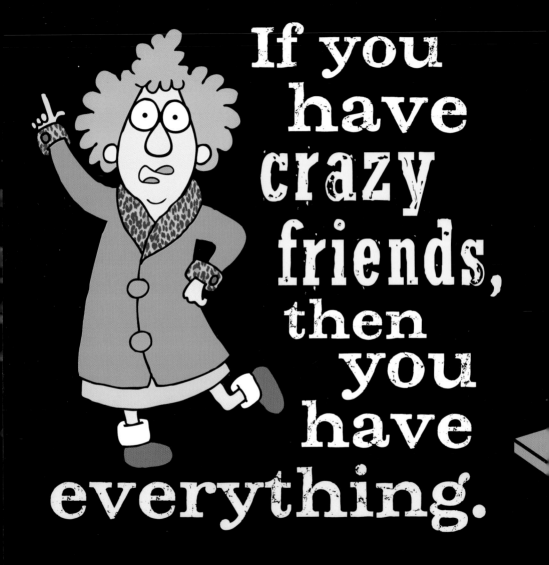

The problem with coffee is trying to MAKE IT when you haven't HAD ANY YET.

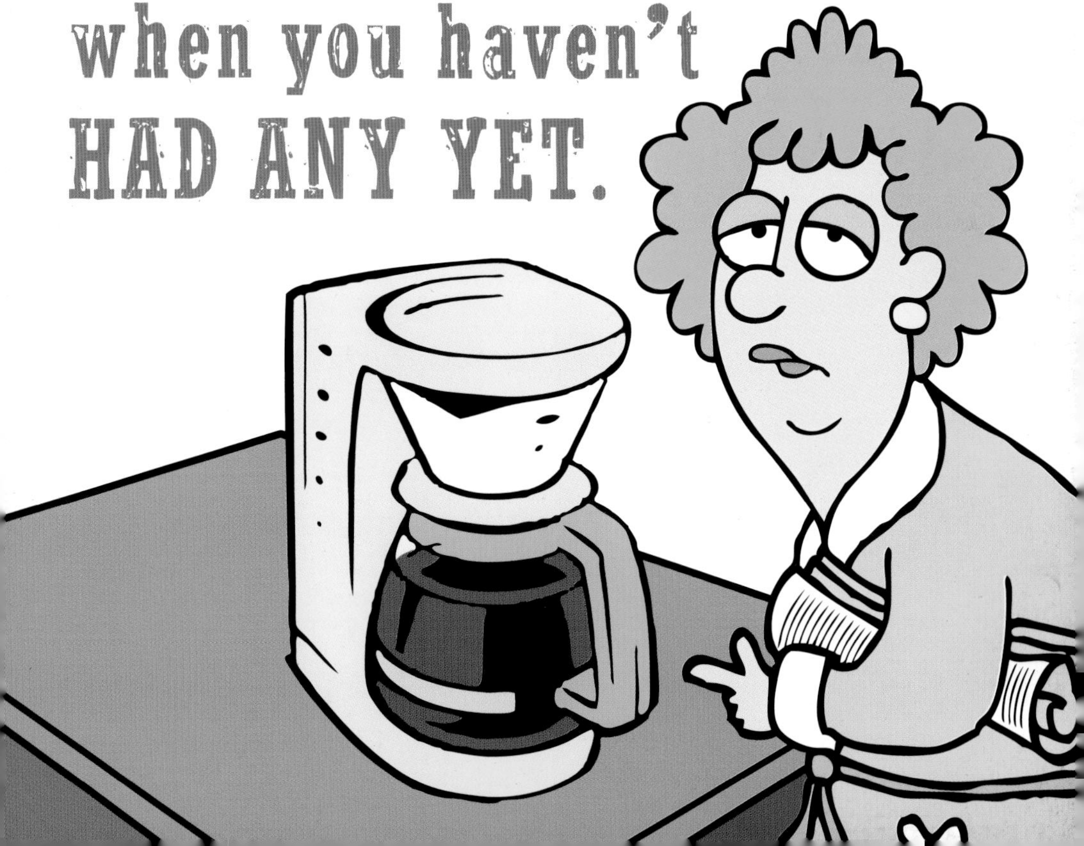

Why do people
with brains
the size of
peas
have mouths
the size of
watermelons?

My day is not complete until I've terrified a total stranger.

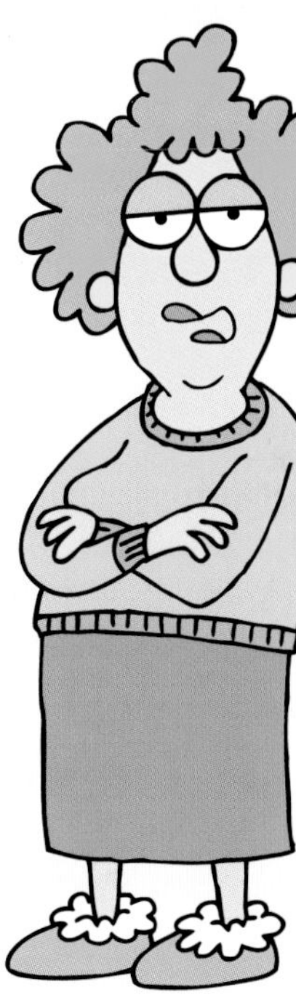

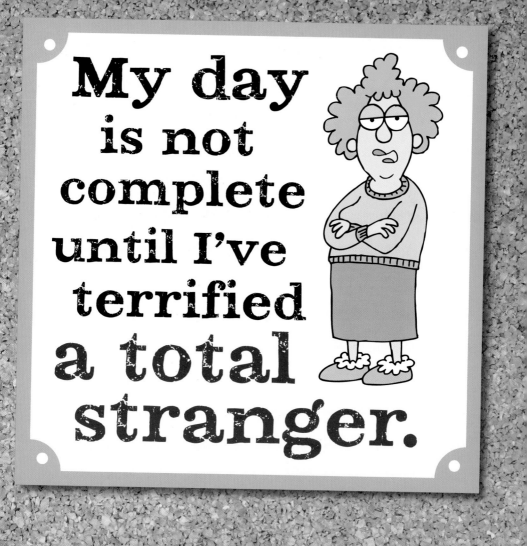

When I get a headache, I take 2 aspirin and keep away from children. Just like it says on the bottle.

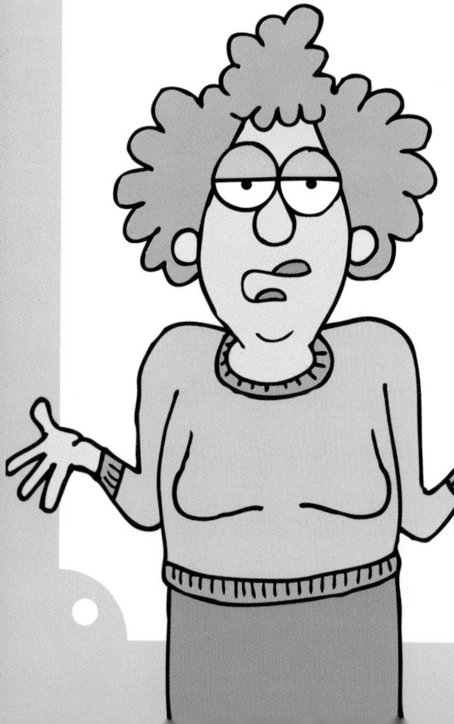

Smile...
It will either
warm their
heart
or
p*ss them
off.
Either way
you win.

Instead of cleaning the house,

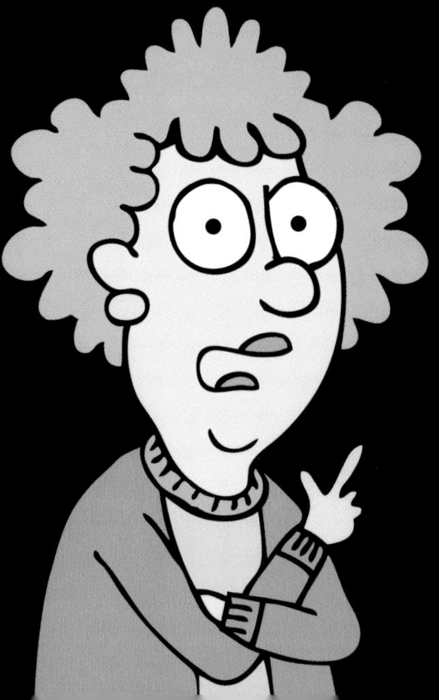

I just turn off the lights.

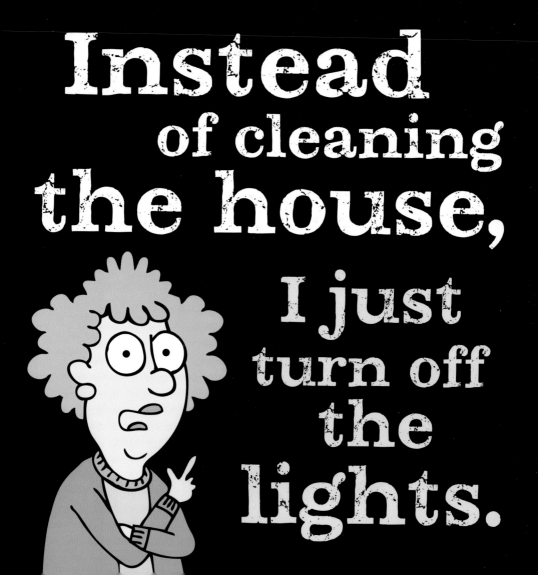

If burglars broke into my house and searched for money, I'd just laugh and search with them.

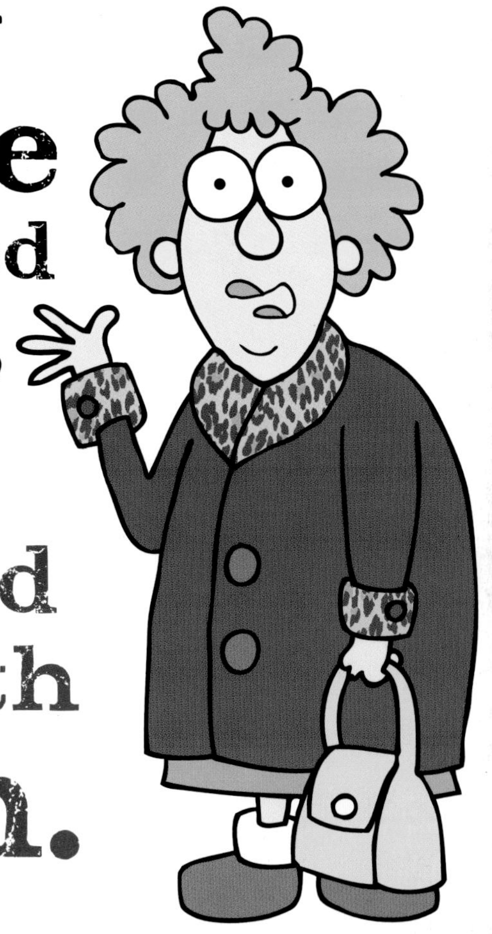

I carry a few extra pounds because it wouldn't be fair to all of the skinny people if I were this gorgeous, intelligent, funny AND skinny.

I'm doing the world a favor really.

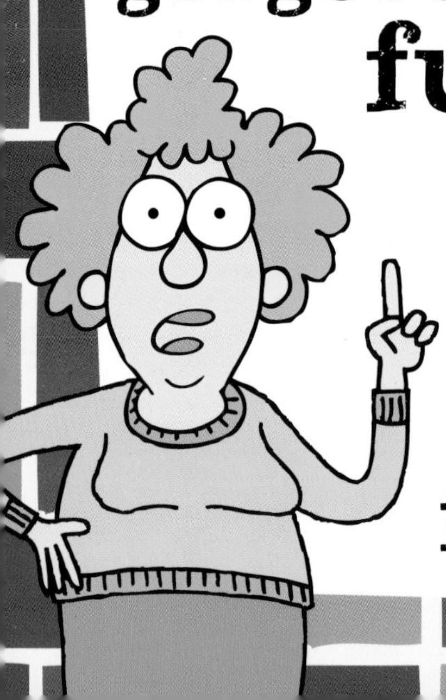

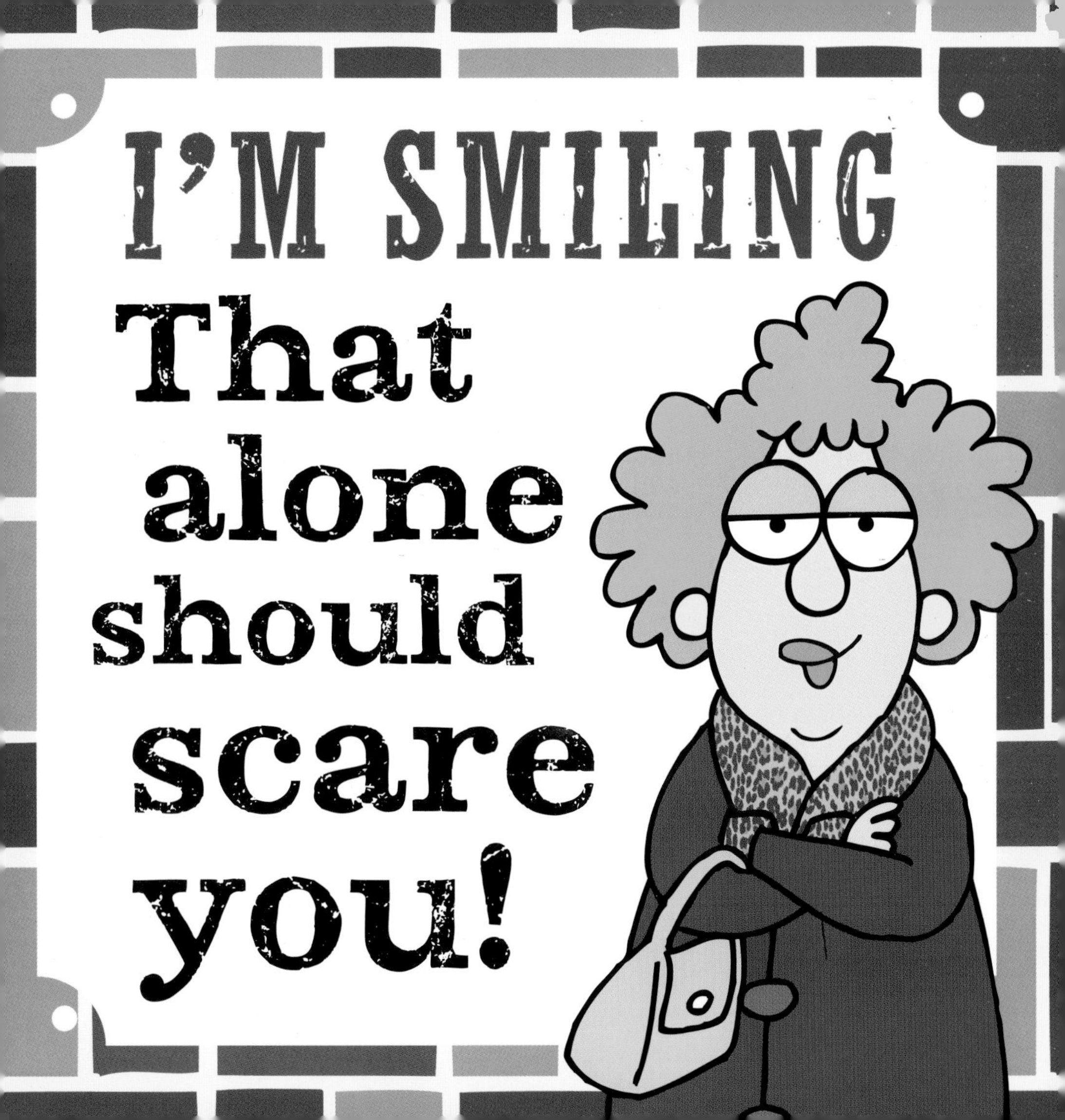
I'M SMILING
That alone should scare you!

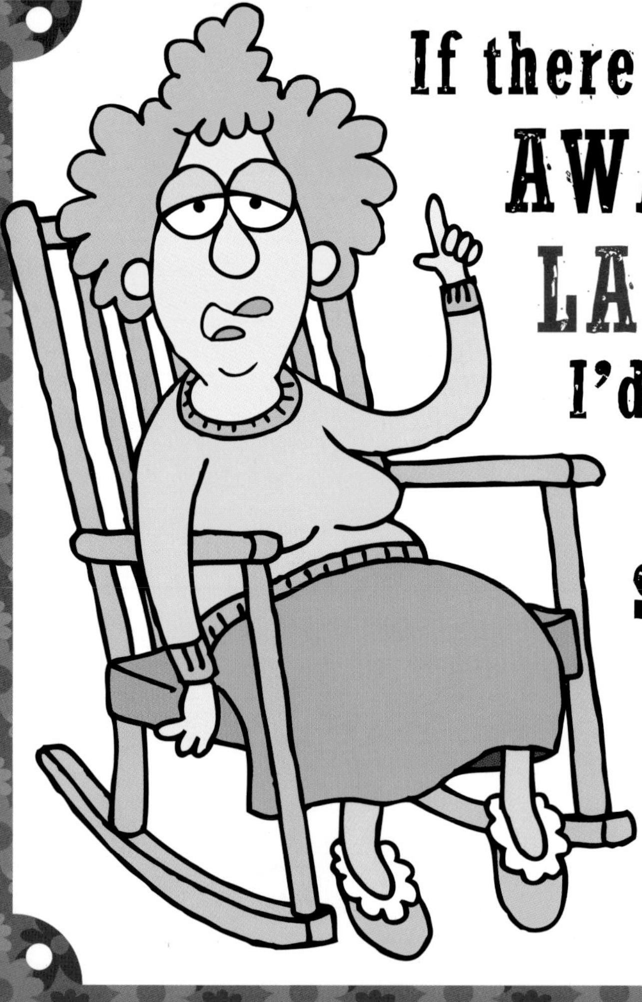

If there was an
AWARD for
LAZINESS
I'd probably
get
someone
else to
pick it up
for me.

Phones face down,
stacked on the table
during a meal...
First person to check their
phone, pays the bill.
Awesome idea!

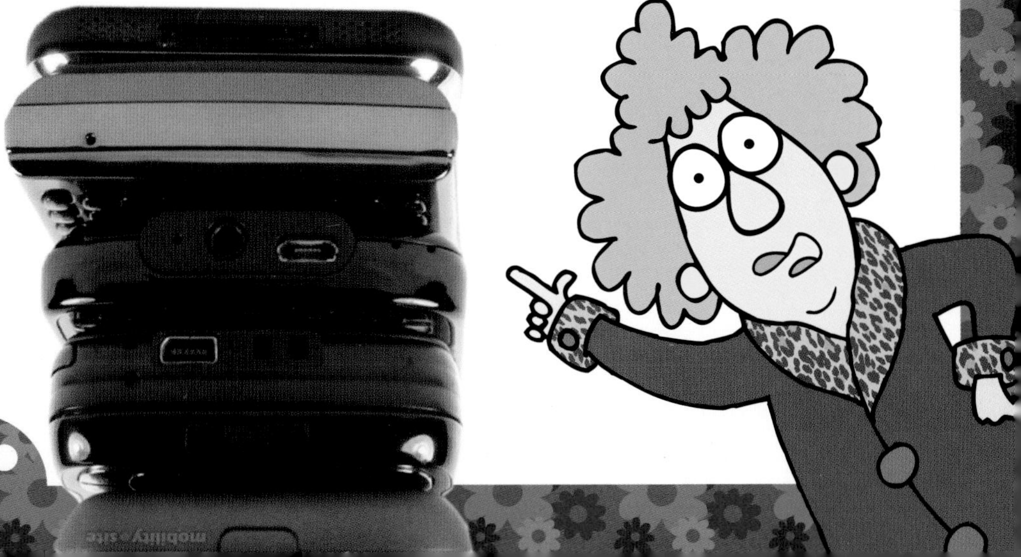

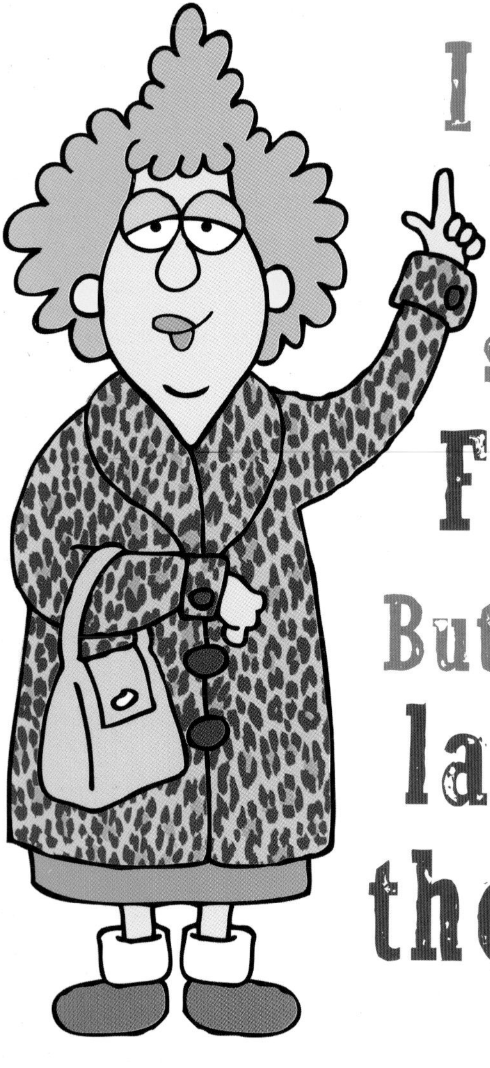

I would
unfriend
some people on
Facebook...
But I enjoy
laughing at
their lives!

SHARE THIS

if you know **someone** who is alive today **simply** because you don't want to go to prison.

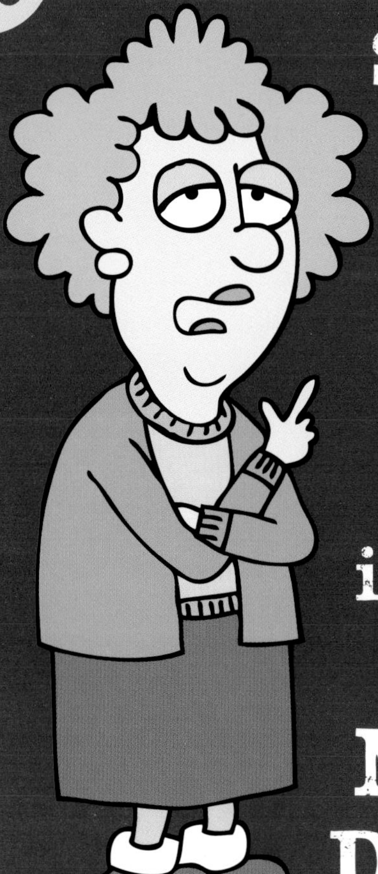

Some days the supply of available **SWEAR WORDS** is insufficient to **MEET MY DEMANDS.**

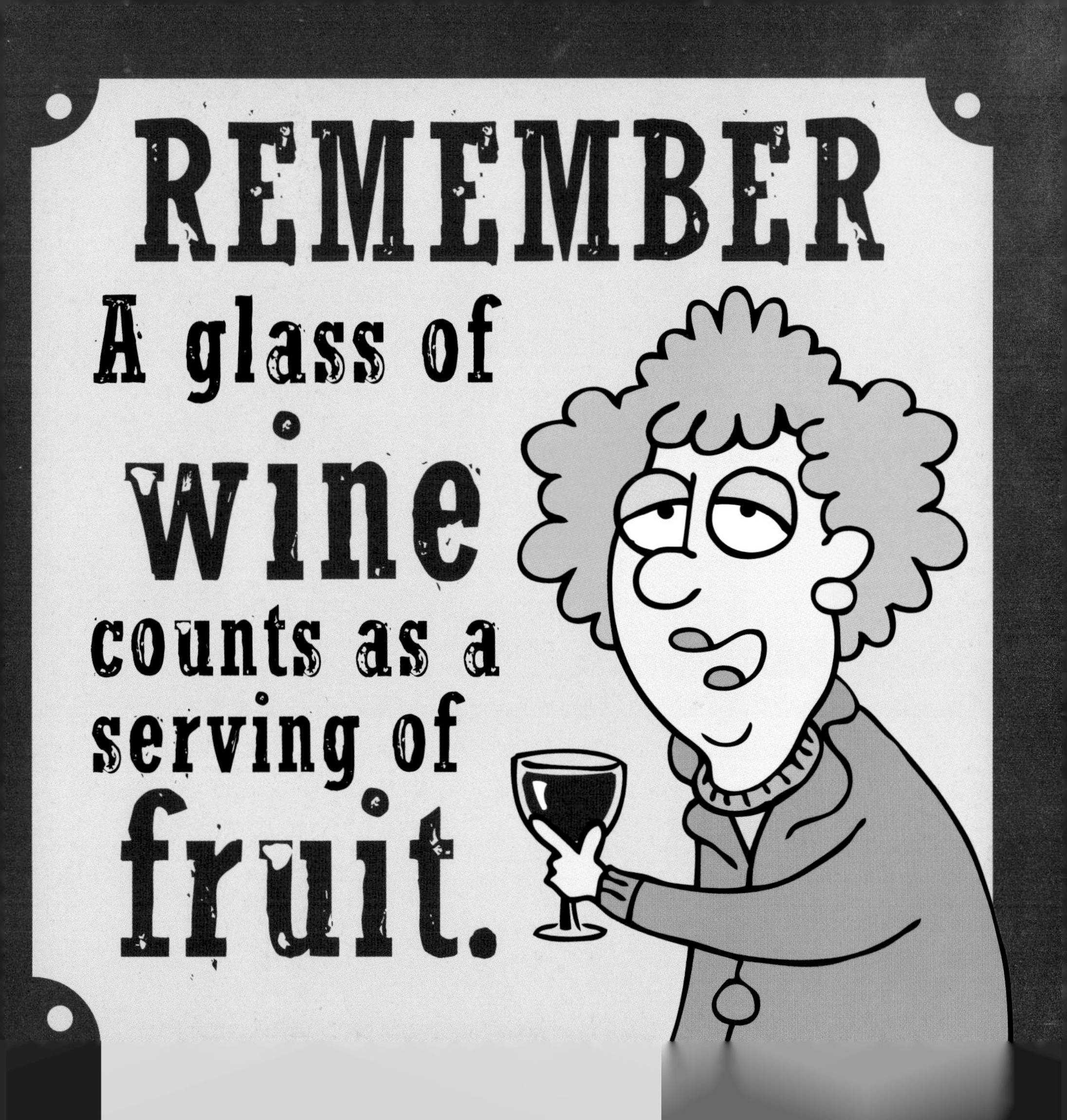
REMEMBER
A glass of
wine
counts as a
serving of
fruit.

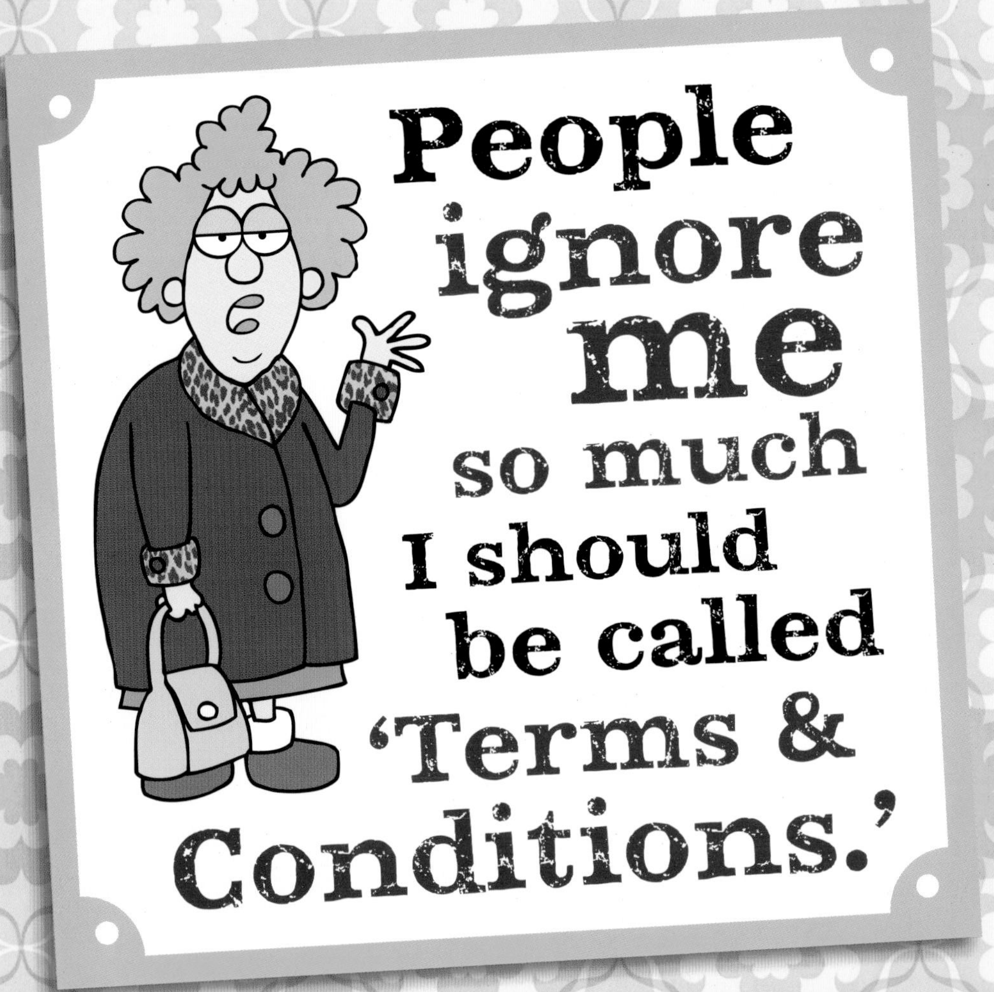
People ignore me so much I should be called 'Terms & Conditions.'

Dear LOL,
Thanks
for being
there
when I'm
stuck for
something
to say.

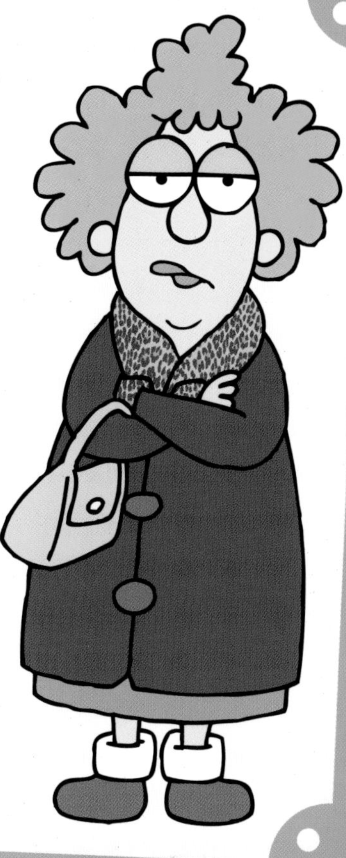

I never use my TURN SIGNAL.

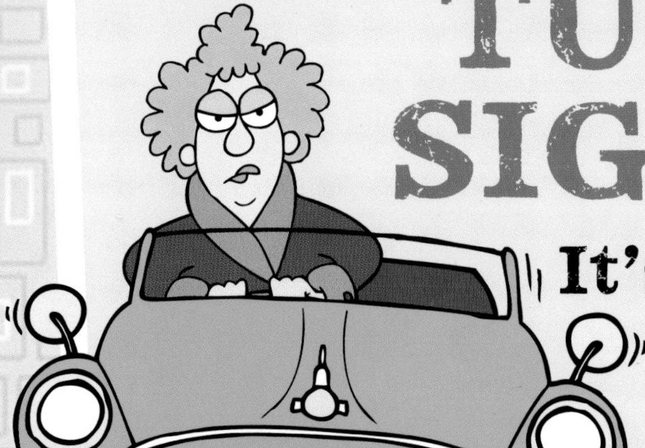
AA1

It's nobody's business where I'm freakin' going.

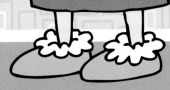

Some people are like freakin' smoke detectors—Loud and really annoying.

The best place to hide a body is page 2 of Google search results.

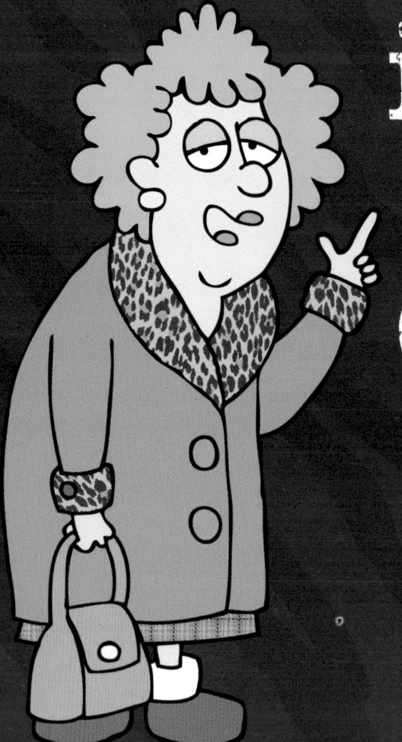

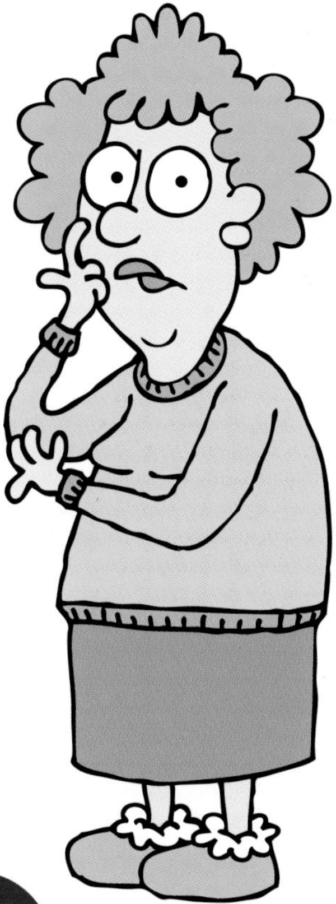

My fake plants
died
because
I forgot to
pretend to
water
them.

ME? NORMAL?
HOW DARE YOU
INSULT ME LIKE THAT...

It's not that I have an "attitude problem," it's just that I have a personality most people can't freakin' handle.

Saying that, I'm not totally useless. I can always be used as a bad example.

Alas, in this big bad world I always try to stay positive. You know what they say: If the cup is only half full I suggest you buy a smaller bra!

You see, if you have crazy friends you have everything, folks—and never forget: A real friend is someone who knows how totally crazy you are but is still willing to be seen out with you in public.

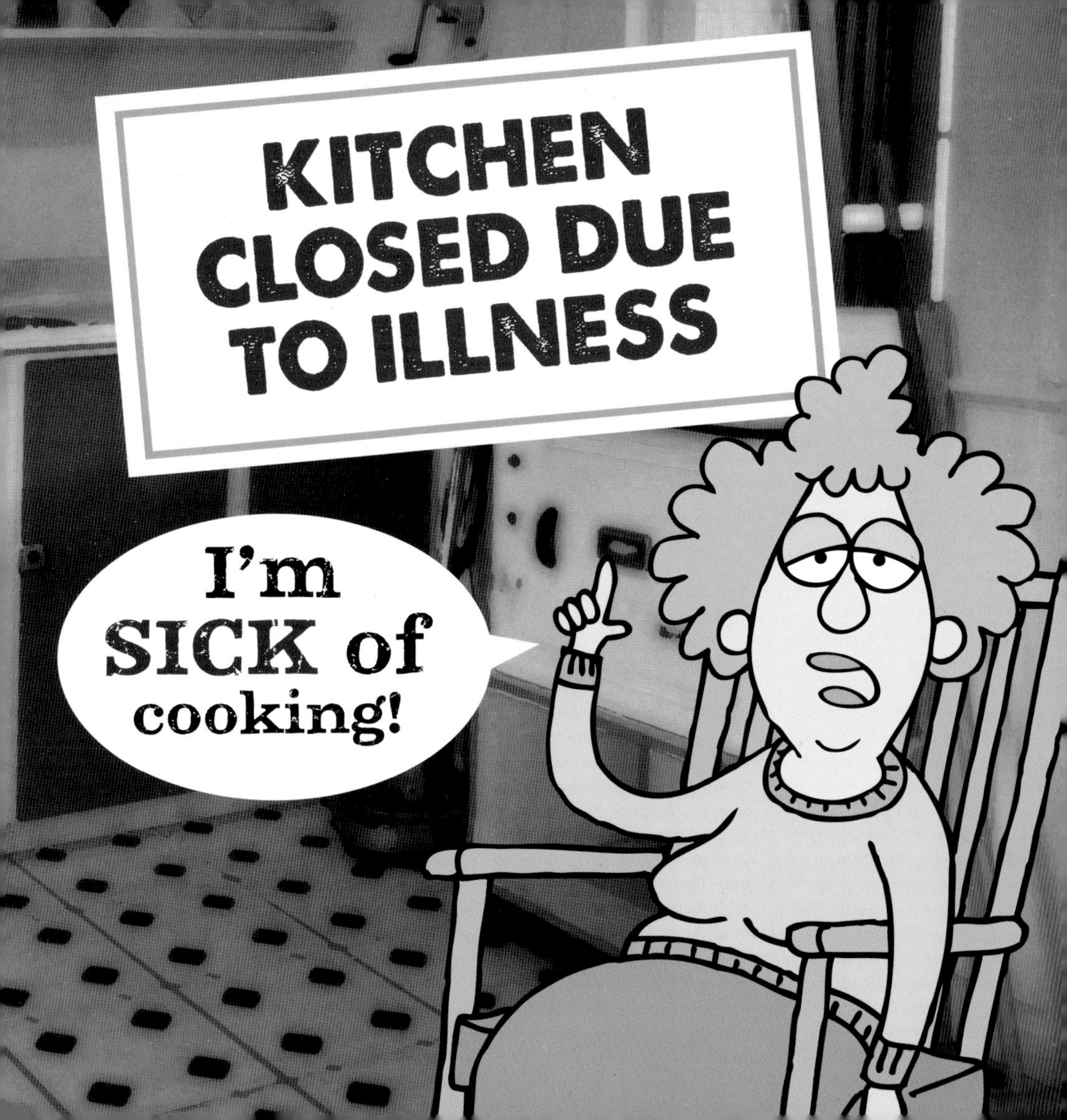
KITCHEN CLOSED DUE TO ILLNESS
I'm SICK of cooking!

If heat makes things expand, I don't have a weight problem, I'm just hot!

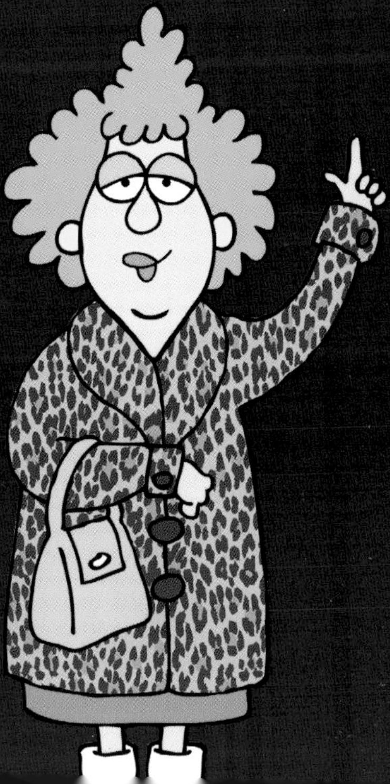

My complete lack of dusting will finally pay off at Halloween.

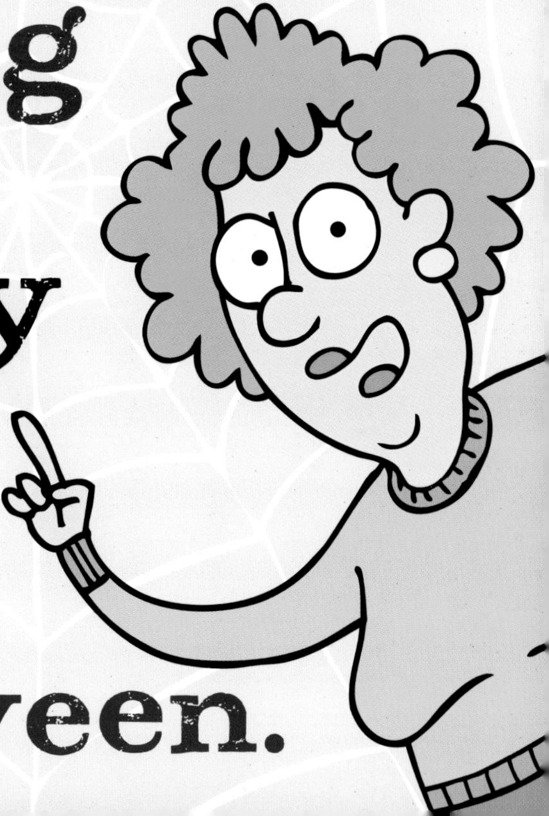

I'm on a light diet. I eat by daylight, I eat by moonlight and I sometimes eat by refrigerator light.

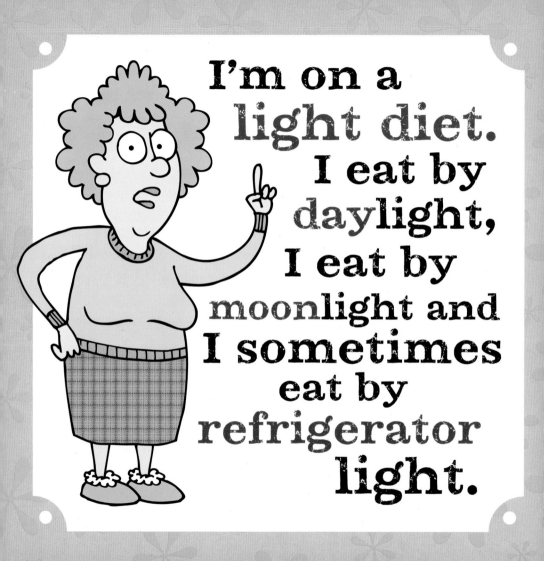

Is your butthole jealous of all the CRAP that comes out of your mouth?

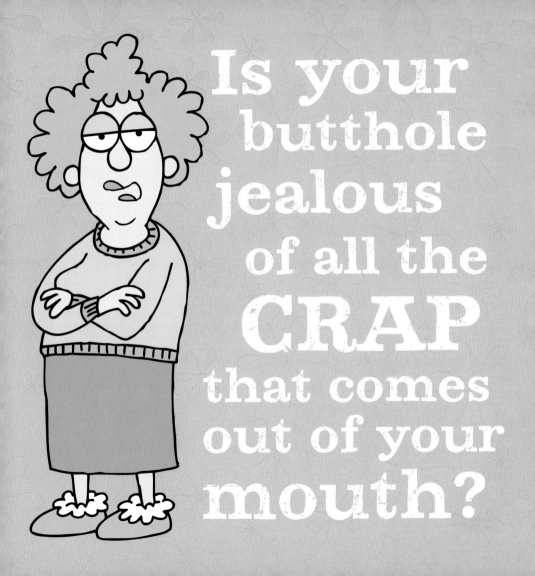

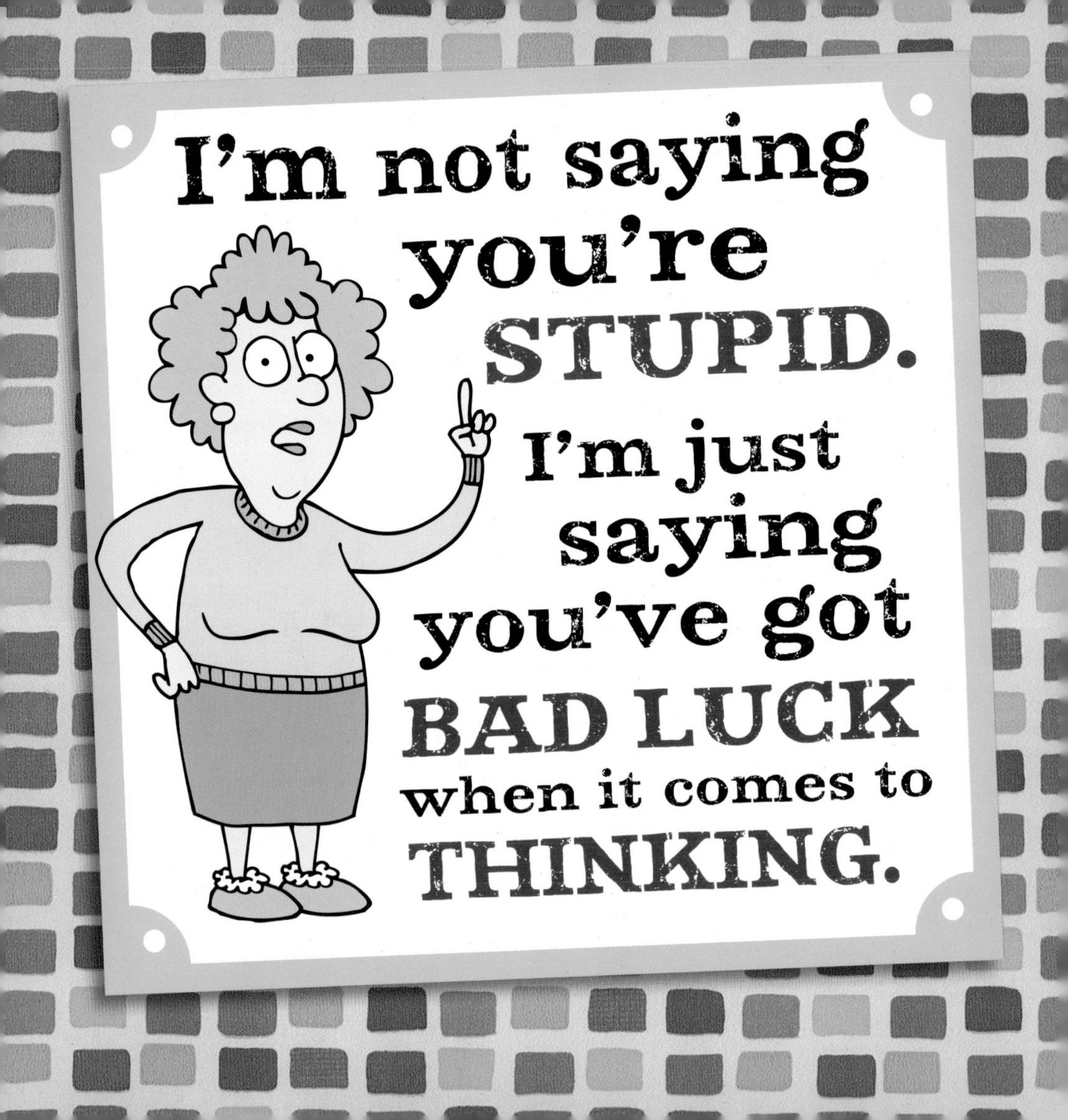
I'm not saying you're STUPID.
I'm just saying you've got BAD LUCK when it comes to THINKING.

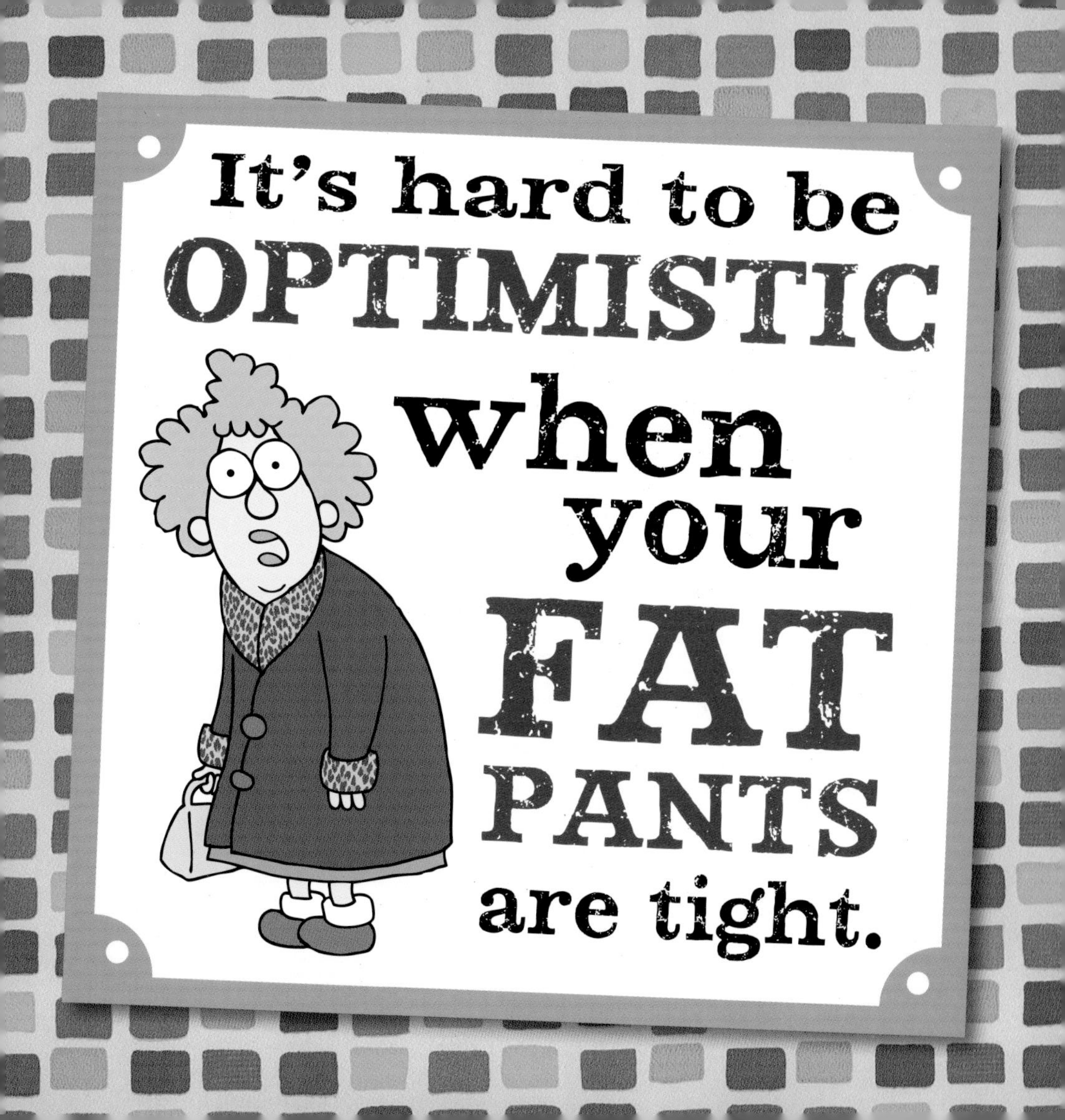
It's hard to be
OPTIMISTIC
when
your
FAT
PANTS
are tight.

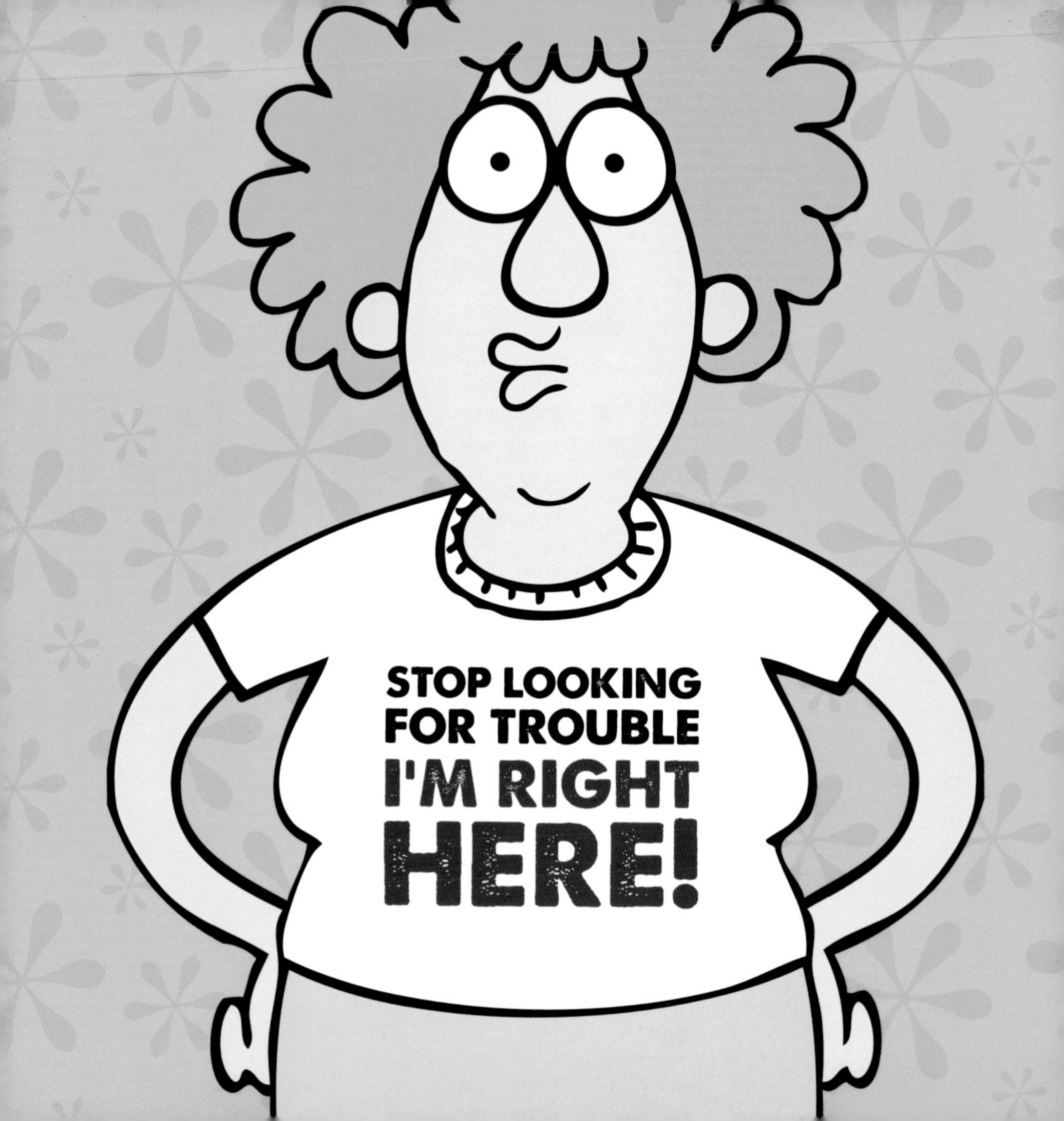
STOP LOOKING
FOR TROUBLE
I'M RIGHT
HERE!

People who say, "Nothing tastes as good as skinny feels" have obviously never had bacon.

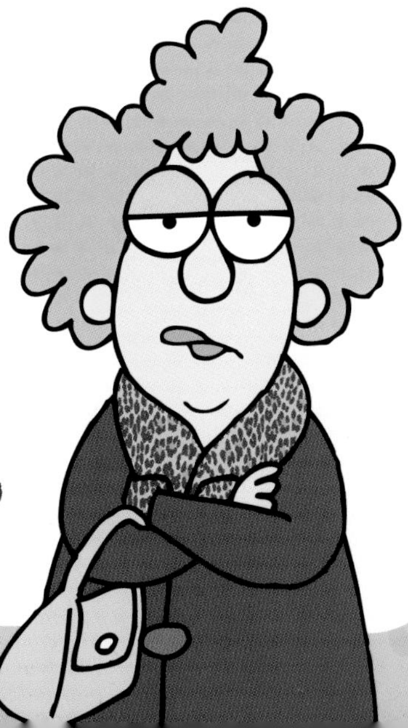

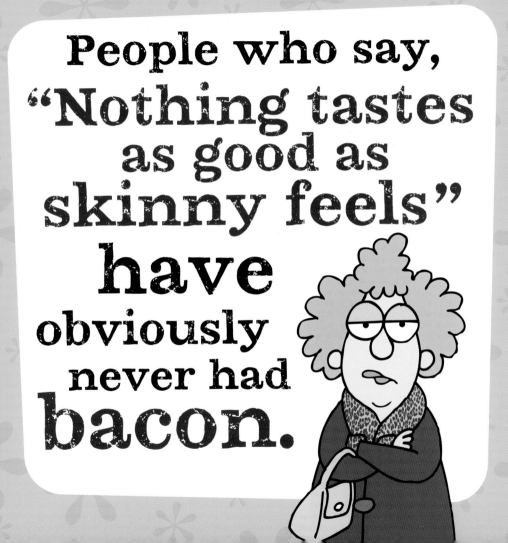

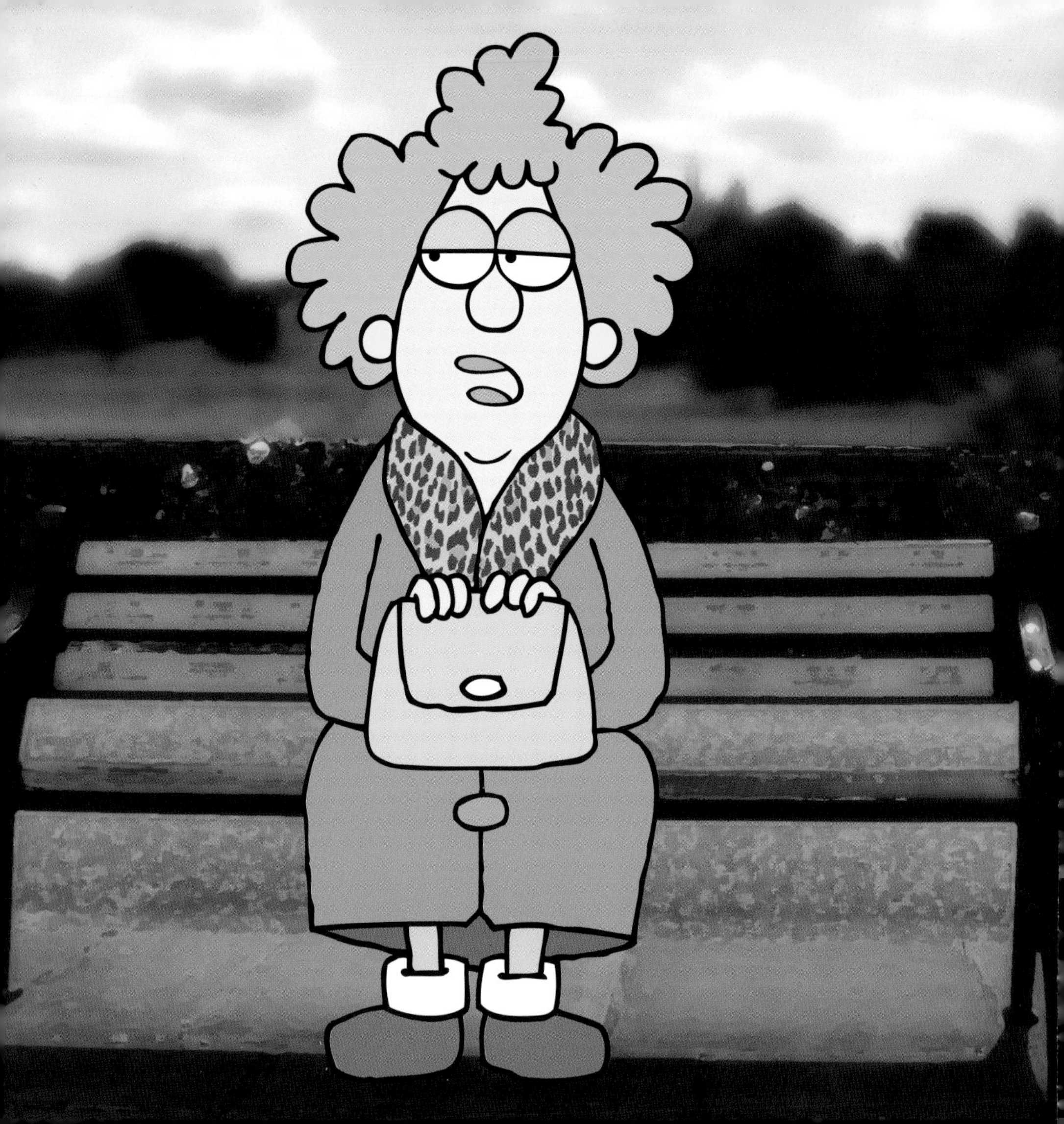

Sometimes
you have to
burn a few
bridges
to stop the
crazies from
following you.

My inner thighs are the **best of friends.** They're just so close.

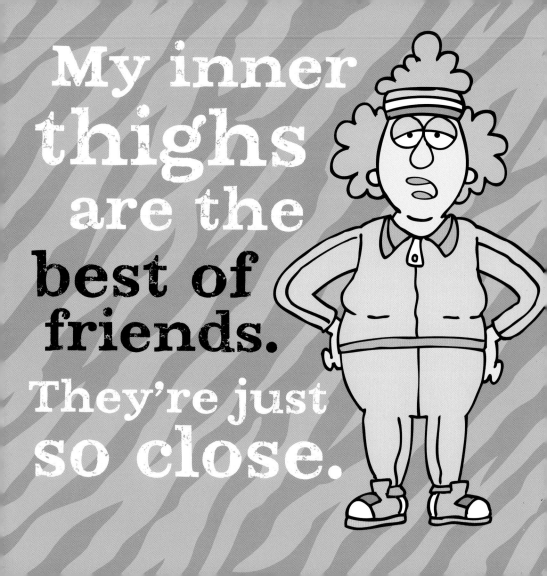

Don't you wish some people would start using glue instead of lipstick?

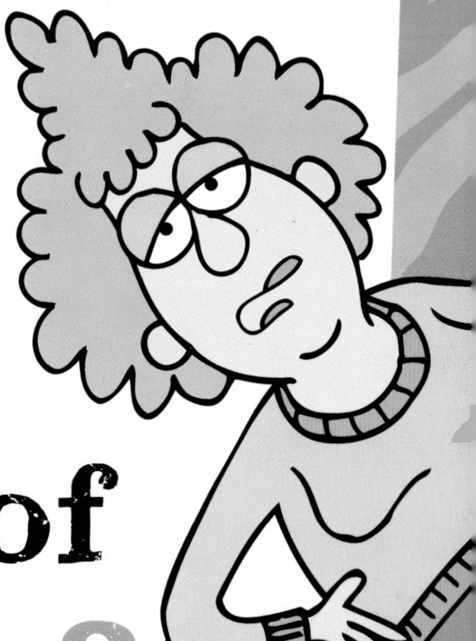

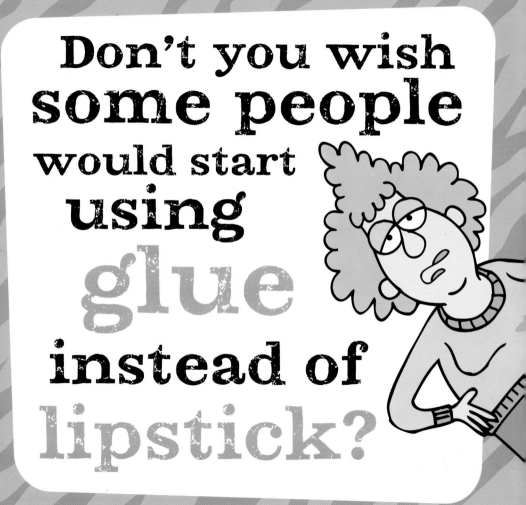

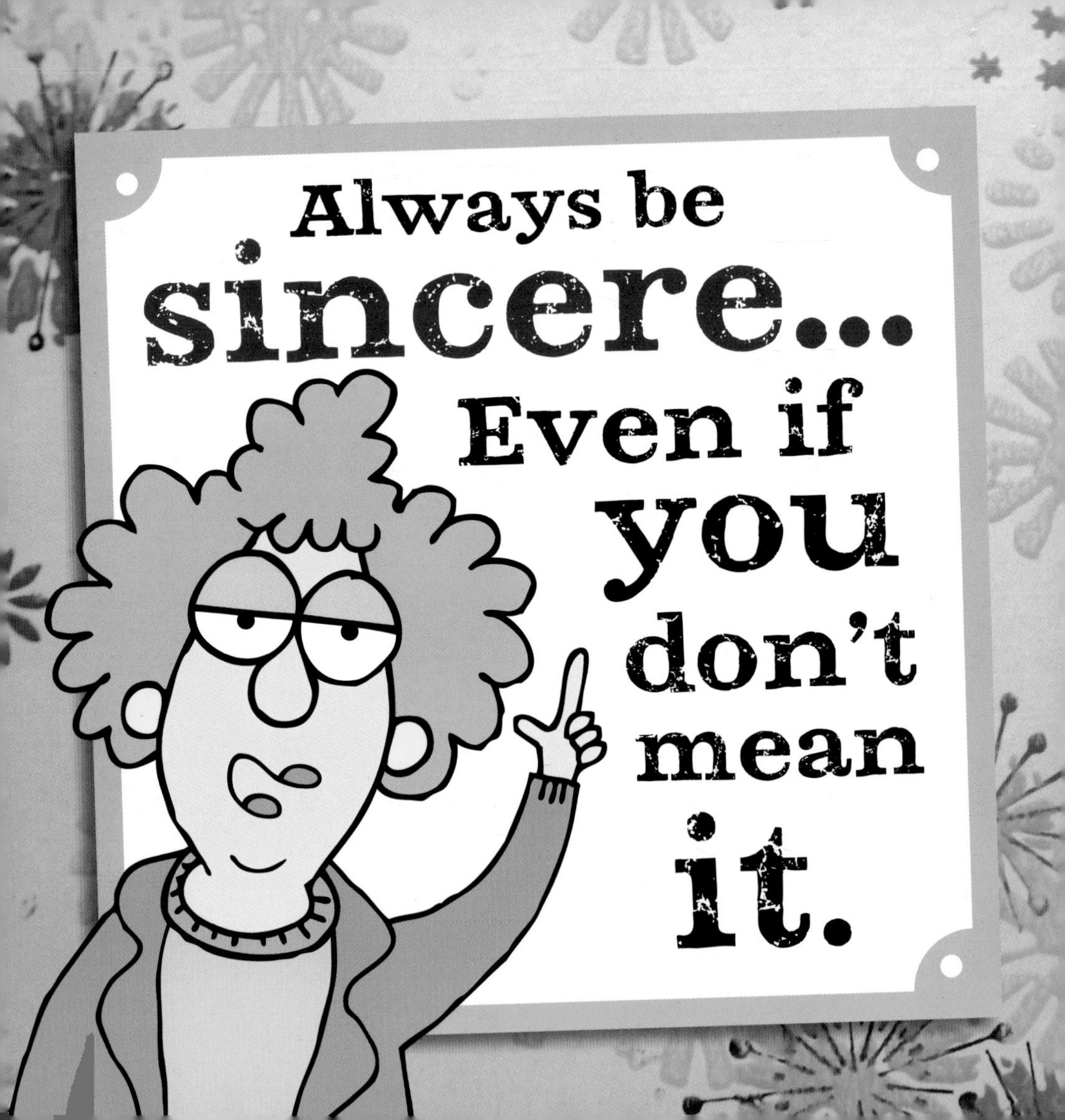
Always be
sincere...
Even if
you
don't
mean
it.

Of course I can keep a secret. It's the people I tell it to who can't!

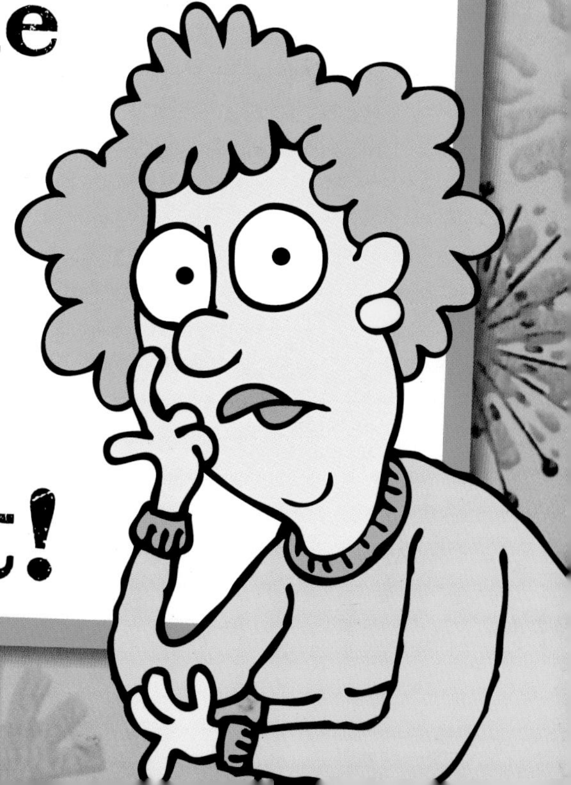

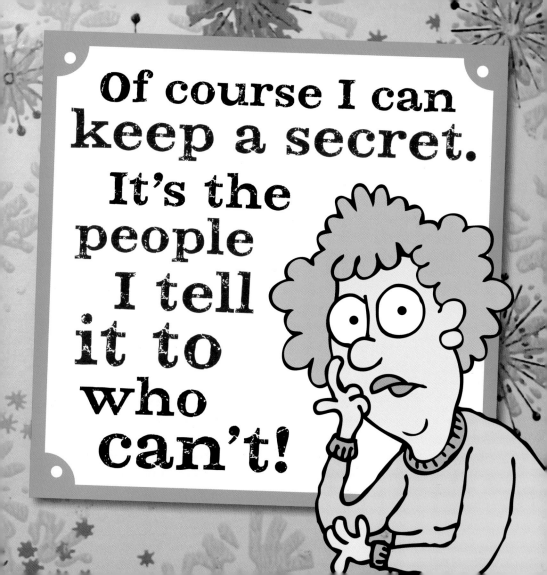

I'm smiling because finally, you've all driven me insane!

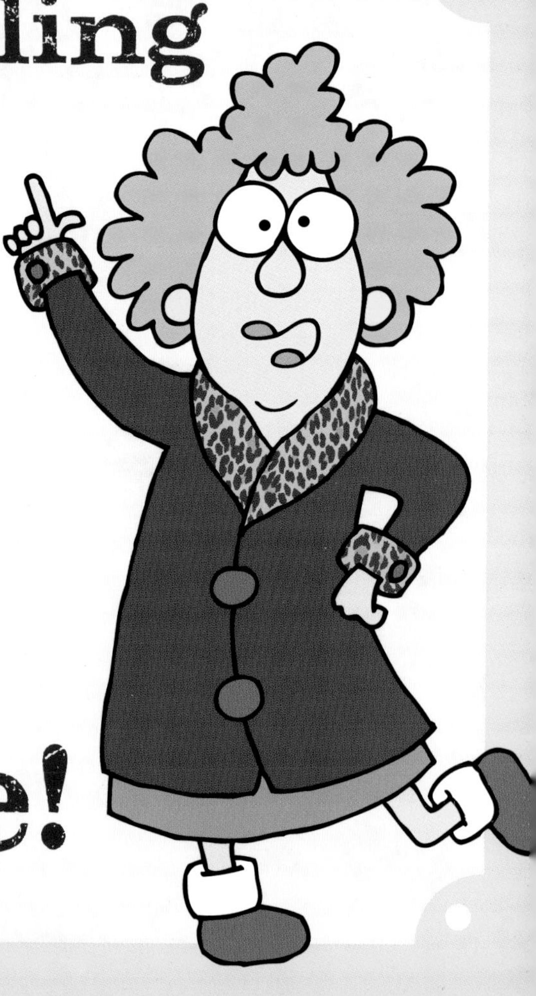

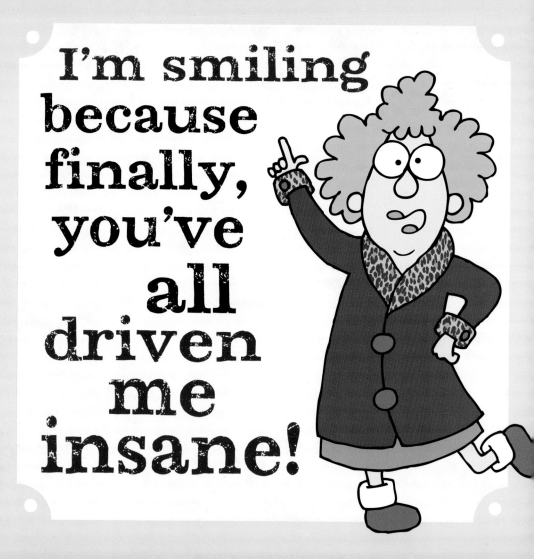

I got a new

STICK DEODORANT

today.

The instructions said:

Remove cap and push up bottom.

I can barely

walk but, whenever I fart,

the room smells lovely.

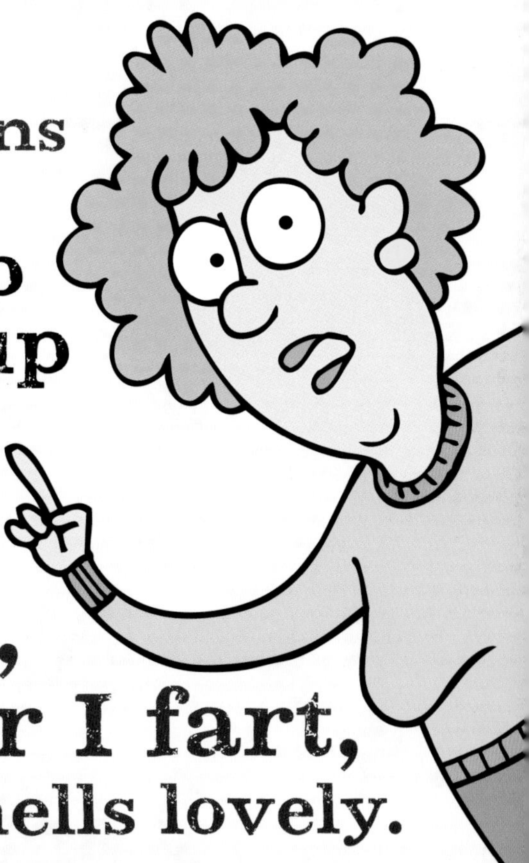

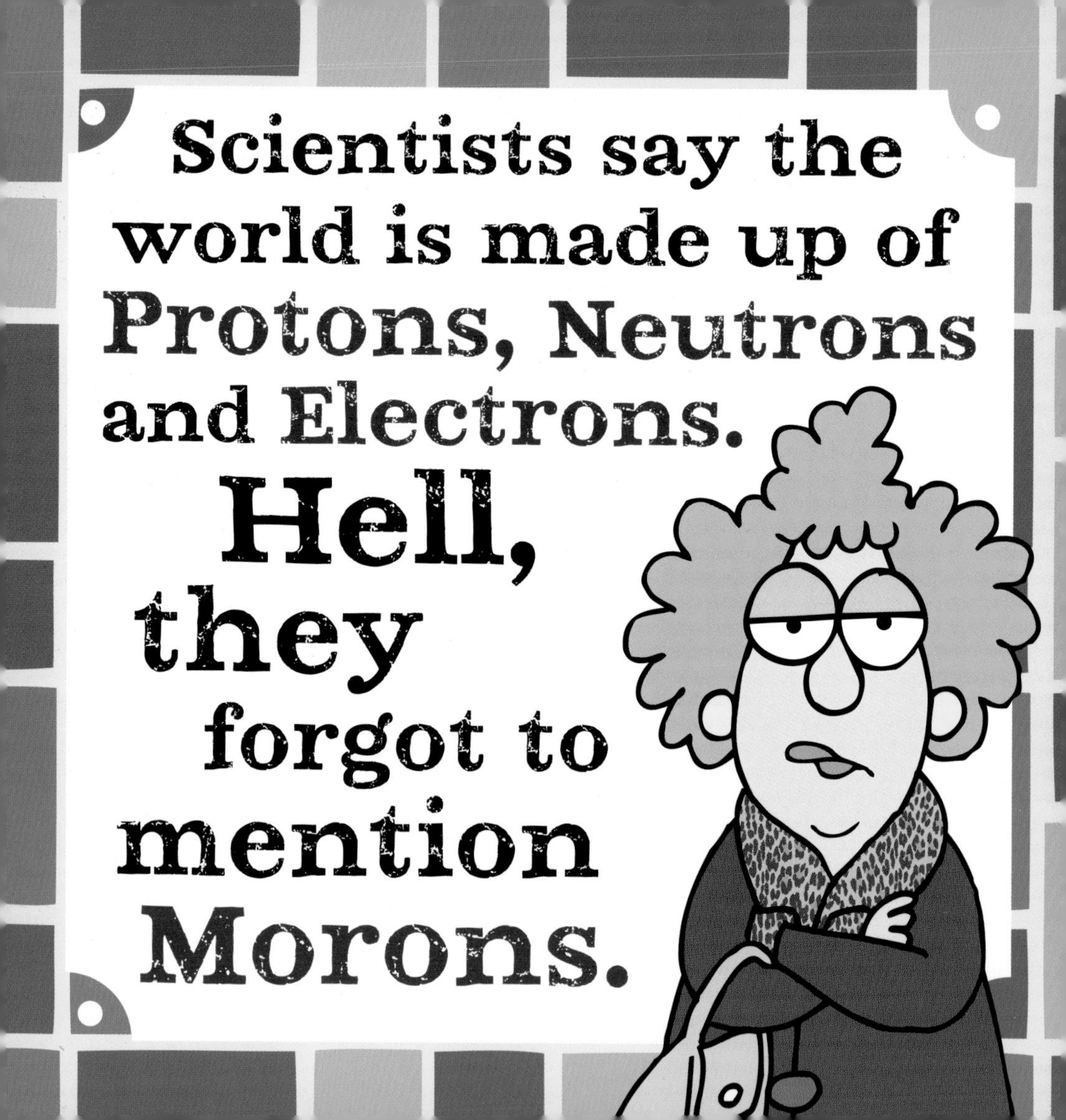
Scientists say the world is made up of Protons, Neutrons and Electrons.
Hell, they forgot to mention Morons.

My friend,
'Normal'
to
US
is just a
setting
on the
dryer.

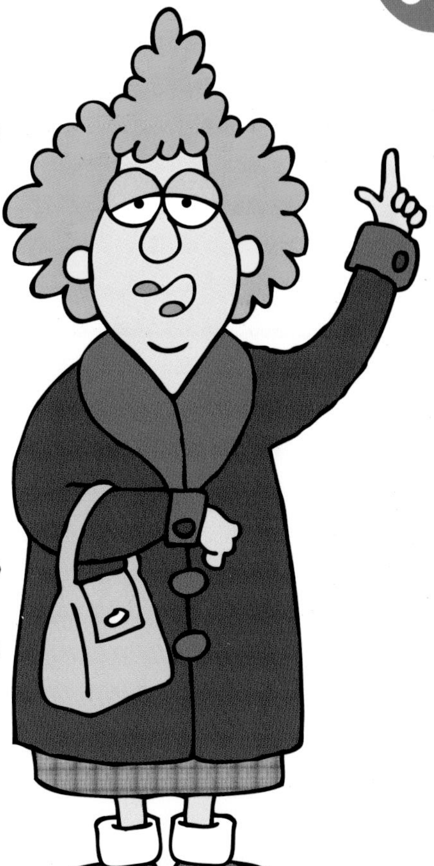

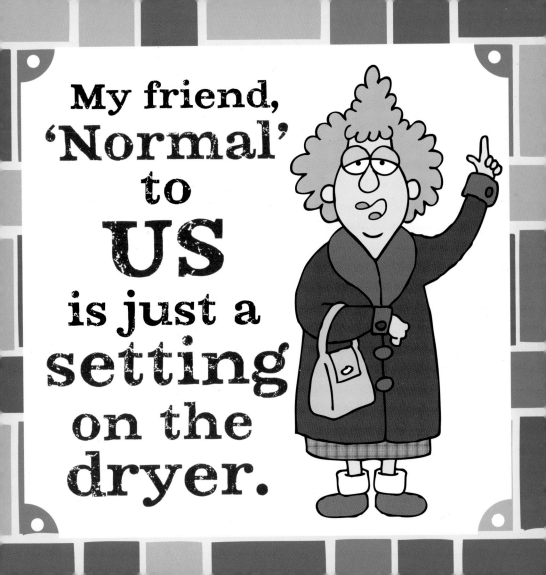

I always offer
two
dinner choices:

1 take it
or
2 leave it

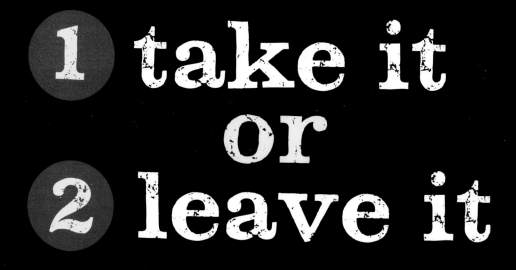

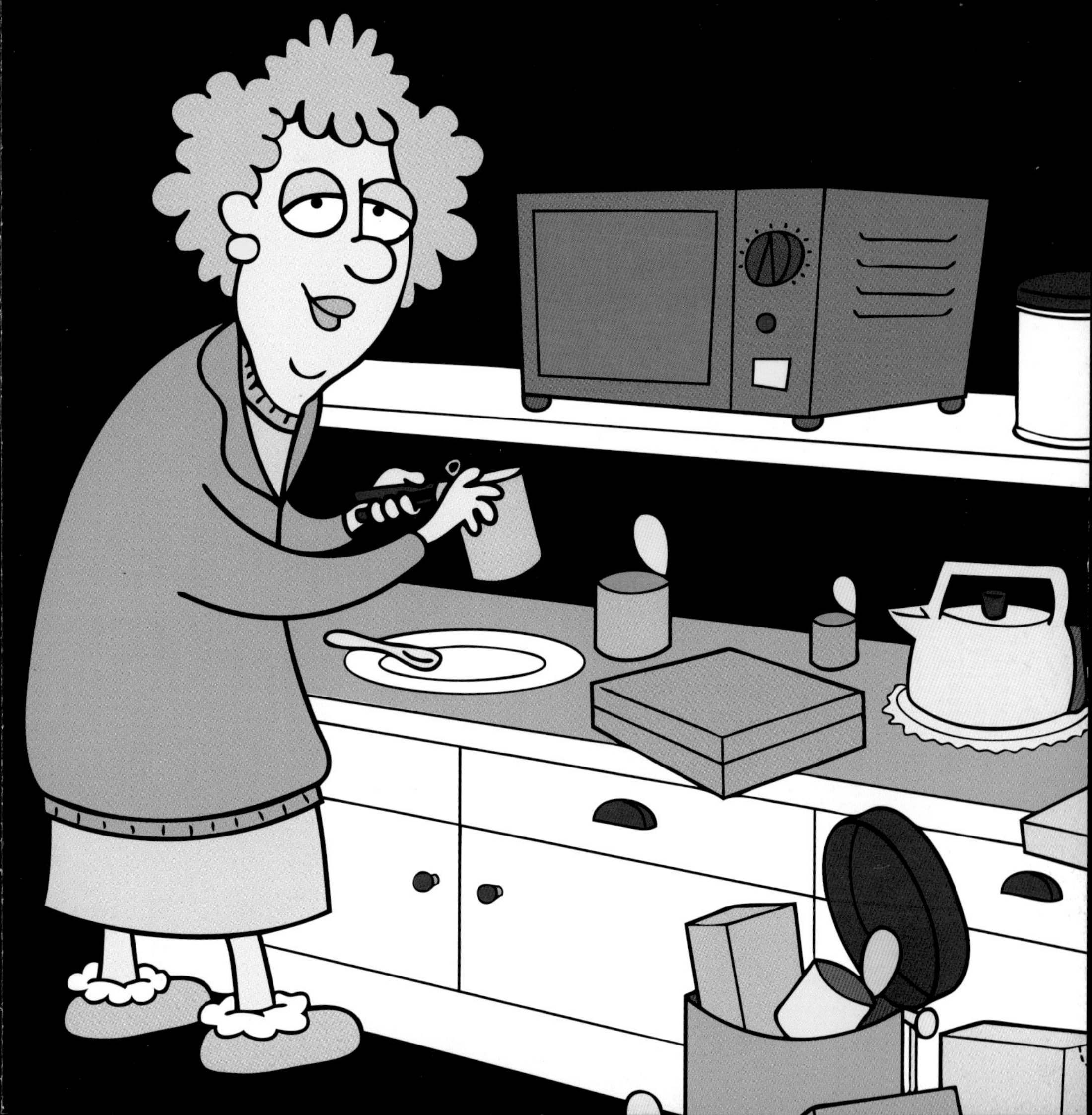

I DON'T LIKE
MORNING PEOPLE
OR MORNINGS
OR PEOPLE...

Don't you think that some people just need a hug... around the neck... with a rope?

You know, I've tried Yoga, long walks, bubble baths, gardening, Prozac – and yet I still want to smack some people. I find it's one of life's great brain-teasers why people with the brains of peas have mouths the size of watermelons – and, yes, it would probably be wise to unfriend these stupid people off Facebook, but I enjoy laughing at their lives too freakin' much.

Read on for some more antidotes to the irritable, smiles for the "tough as old boots" days – and laughs that will hopefully tickle your soul.

When life's idiots are really getting you down just remember that somewhere in this world right now, there's an idiot pulling a door that says push!

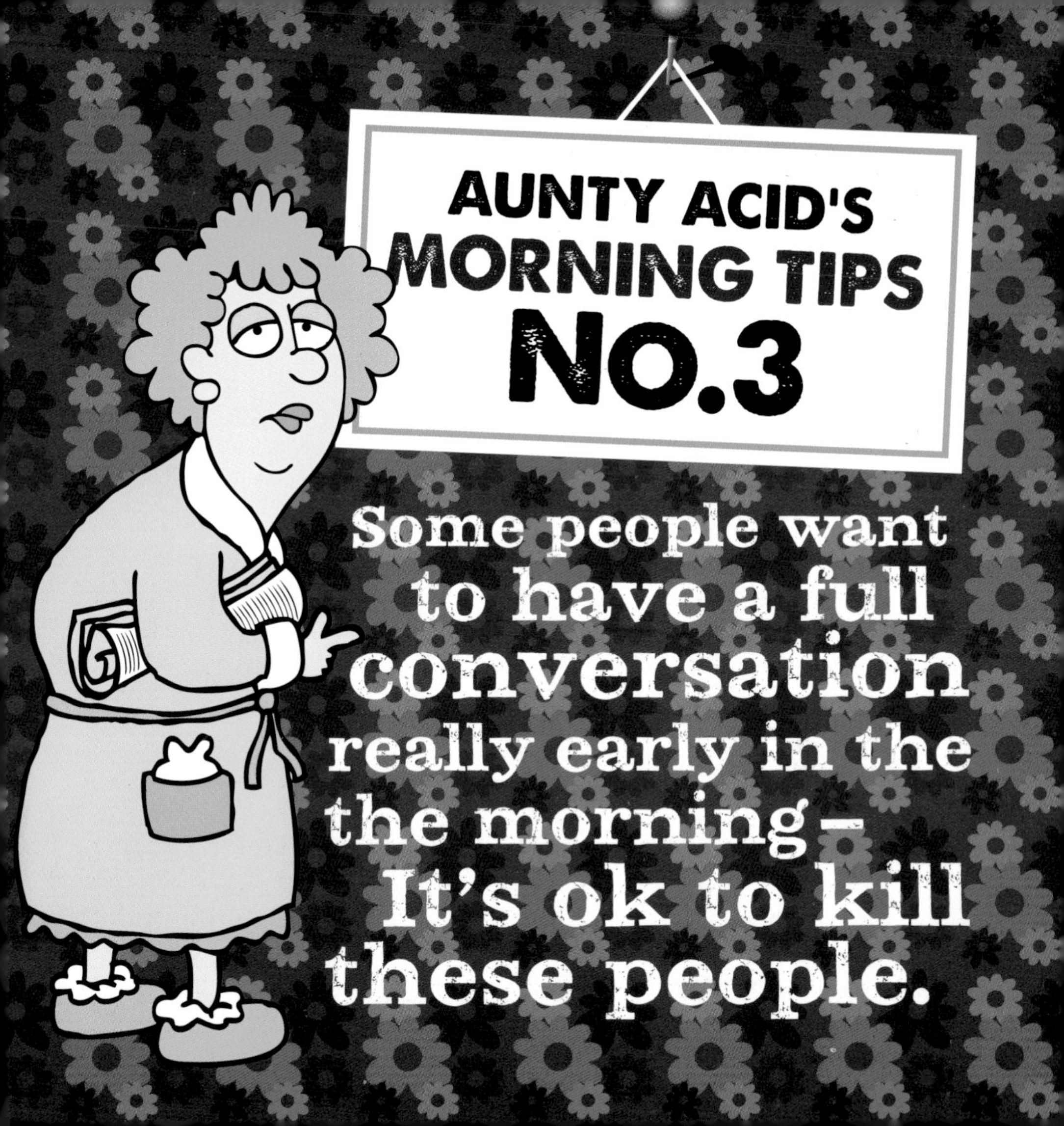
AUNTY ACID'S
MORNING TIPS
NO.3
Some people want to have a full conversation really early in the the morning–
It's ok to kill these people.

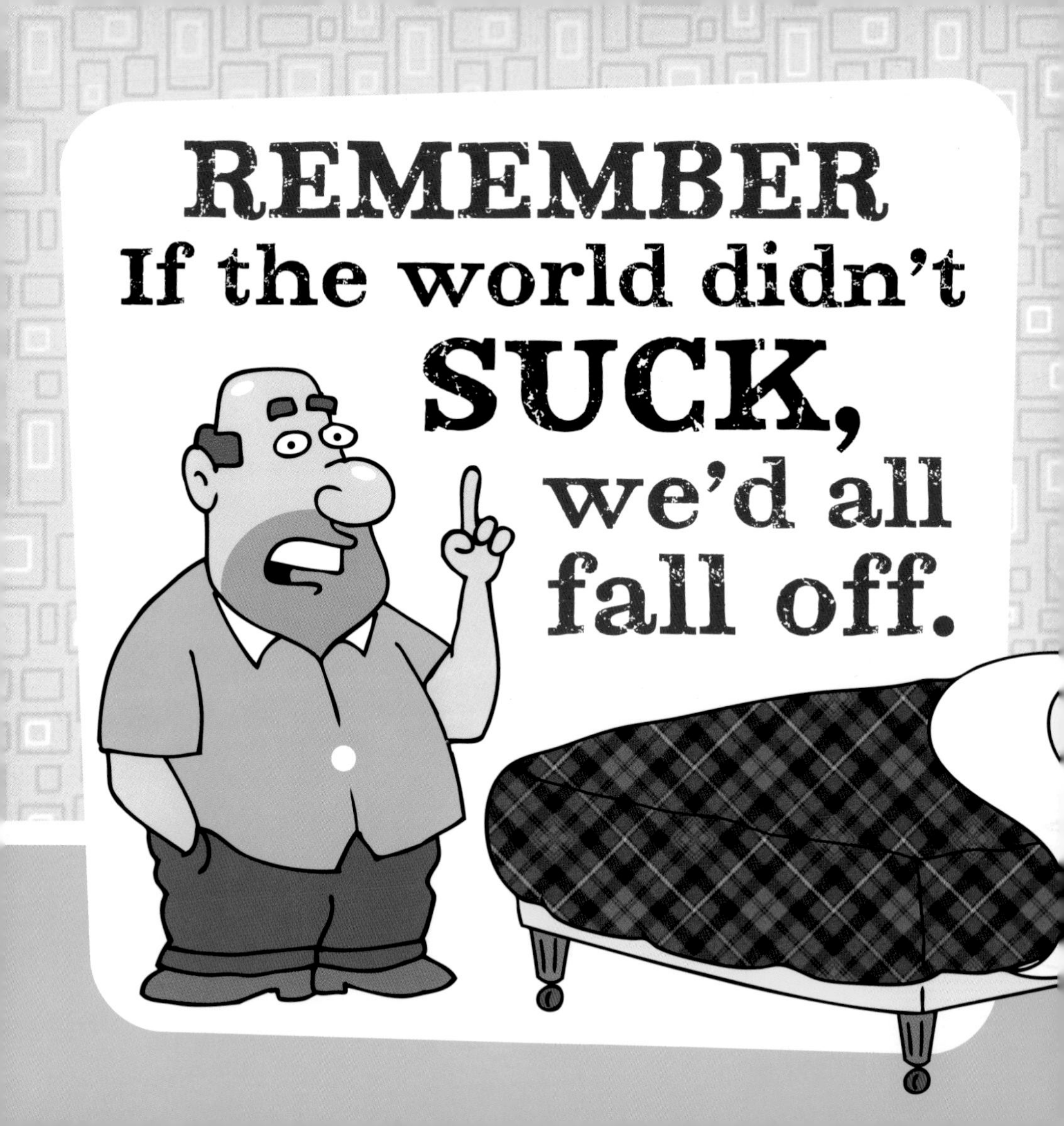
REMEMBER
If the world didn't
SUCK,
we'd all
fall off.

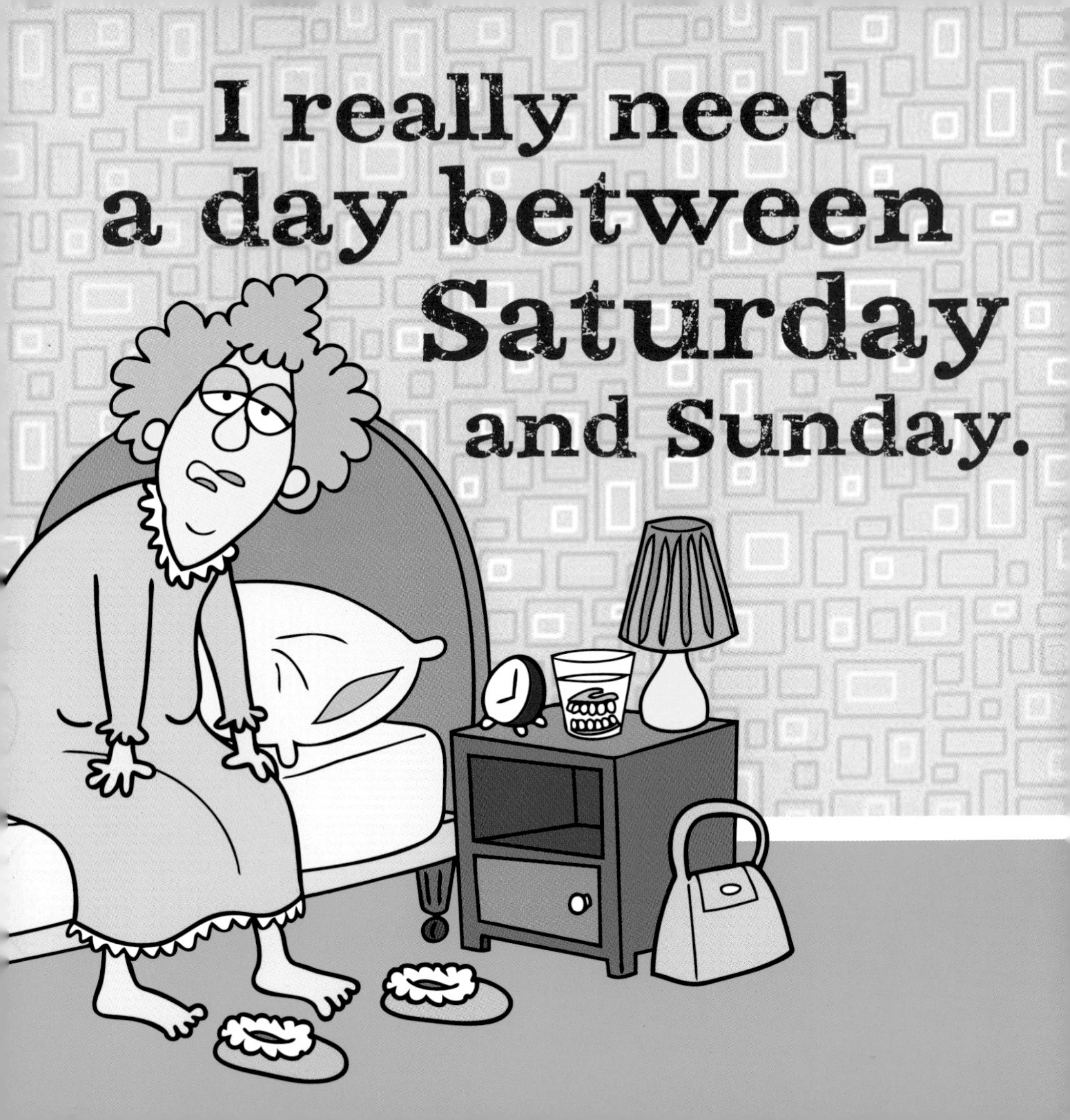
I really need
a day between
Saturday
and Sunday.

I have a condition that prevents me from **dieting.**

It's called being freakin' hungry.

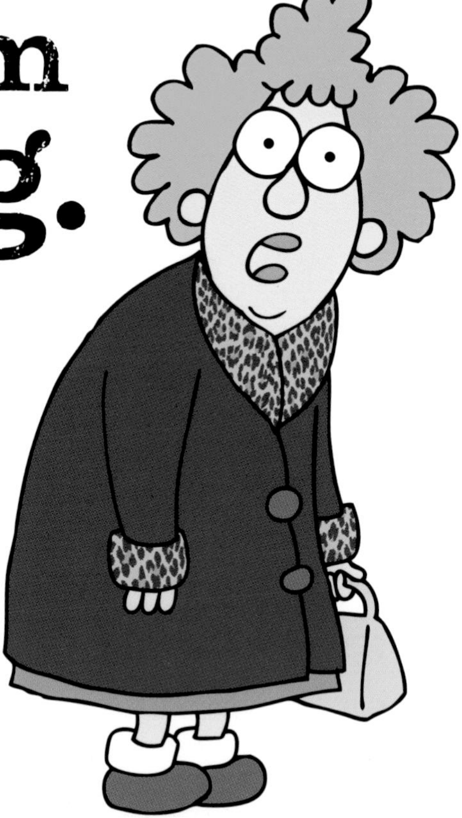

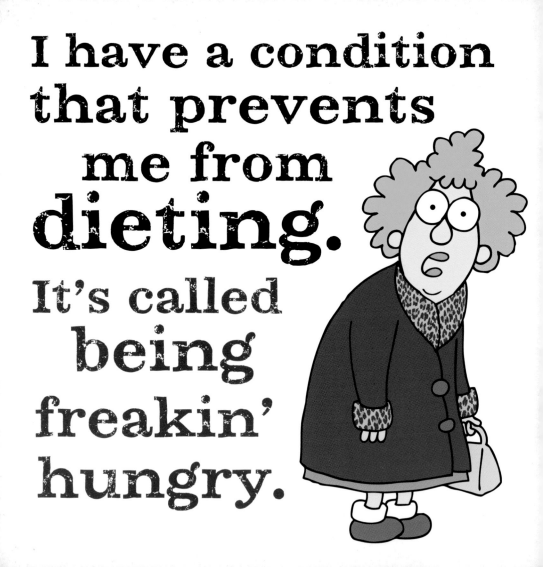

I'm not
an
alcoholic.
Alcoholics
go to
meetings.
I'm a
drunk.
We go to parties.

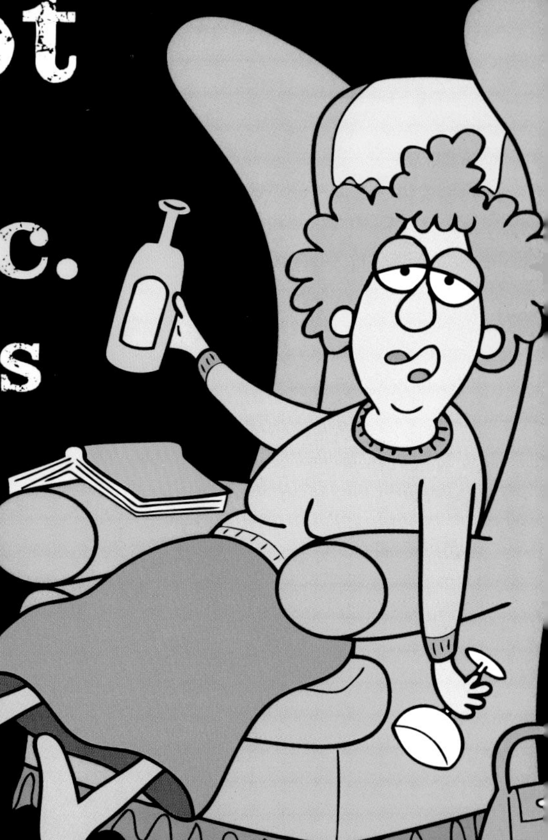

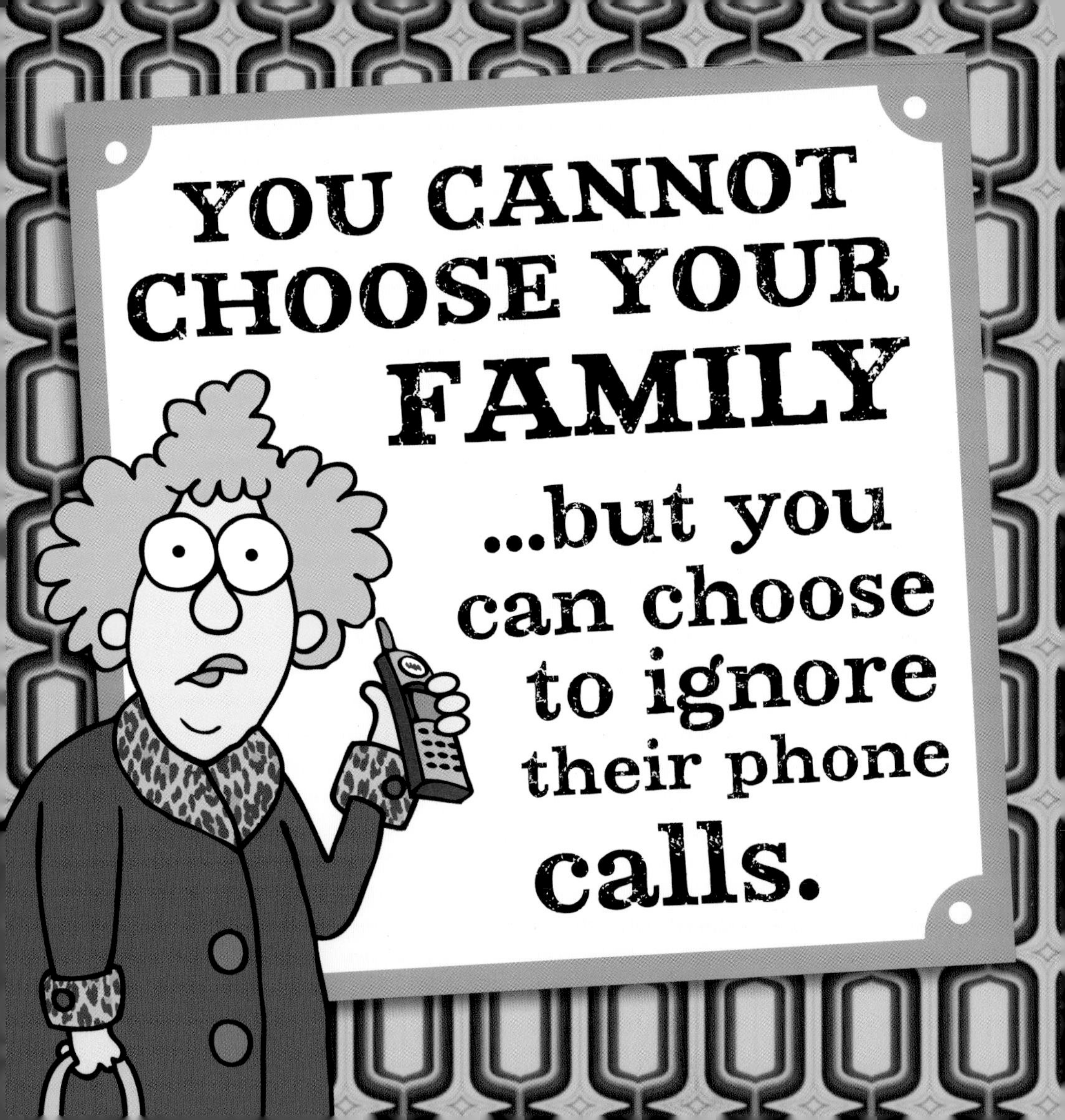
YOU CANNOT CHOOSE YOUR FAMILY
...but you can choose to ignore their phone calls.

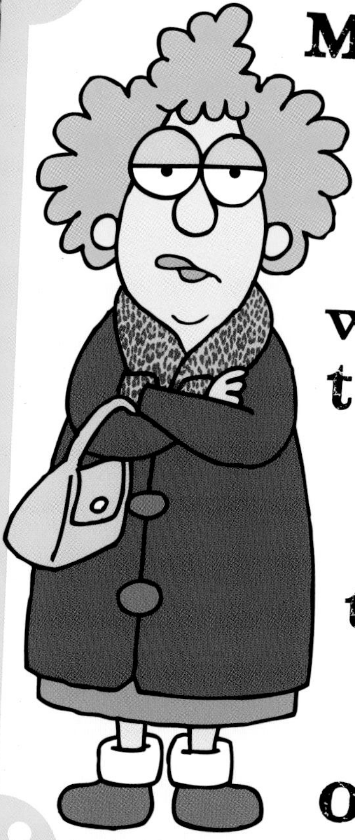

My bank has a **new service** where they will text you your **balance.** I just don't think they should add **LOL** on the end.

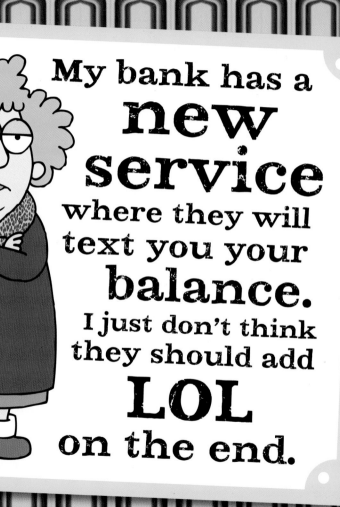

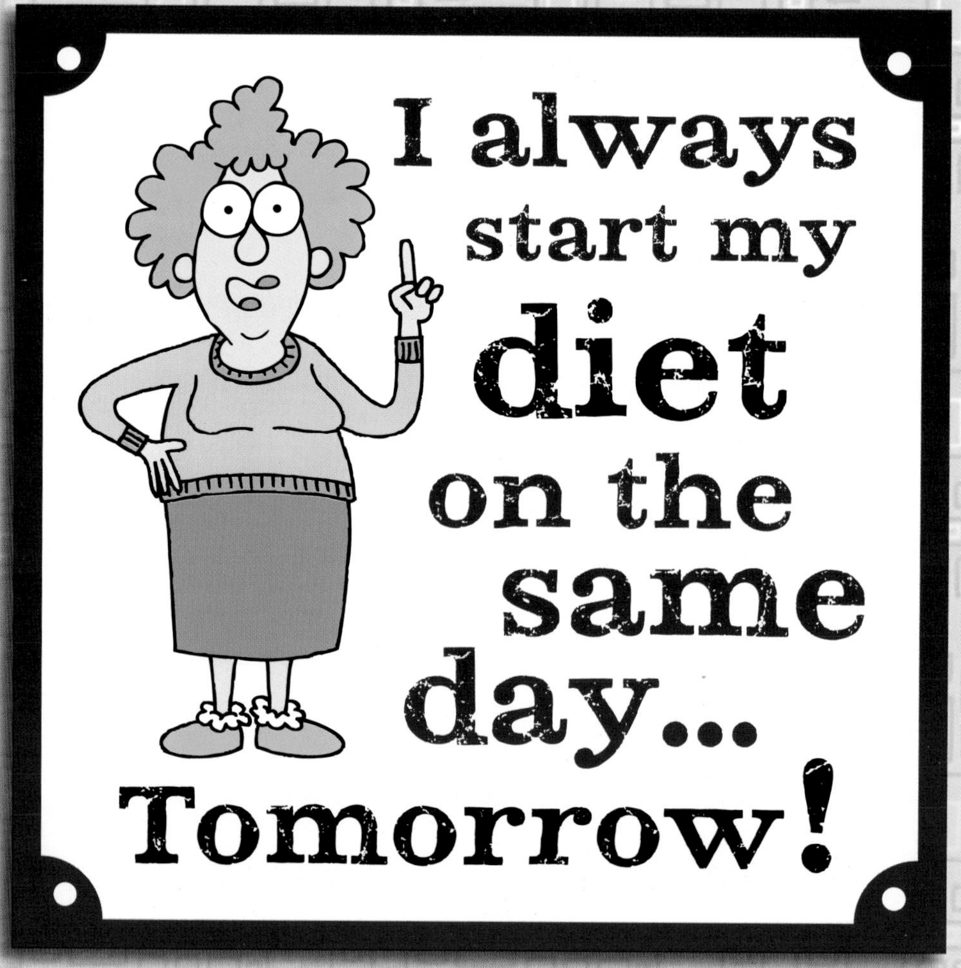
I always start my diet on the same day... Tomorrow!

Read an article titled "How to get Ryan Gosling's body" but it's just a bunch of health tips for men and nothing at all about kidnapping.

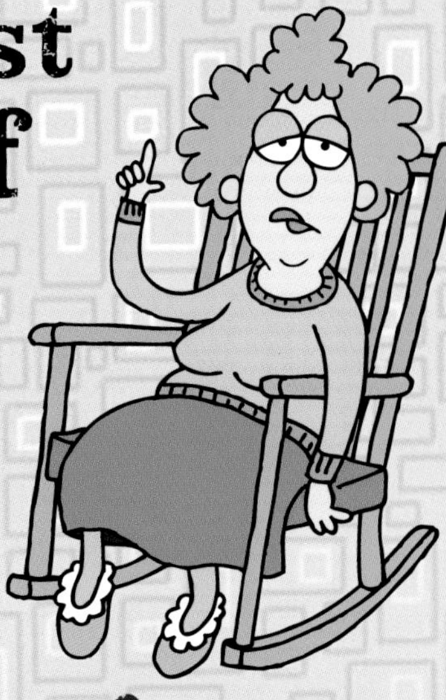

If I died and went straight to **Hell**, it would take me a week to realize I wasn't at **work** anymore.

If we're not meant to have **midnight snacks,** why is there a light in the fridge?

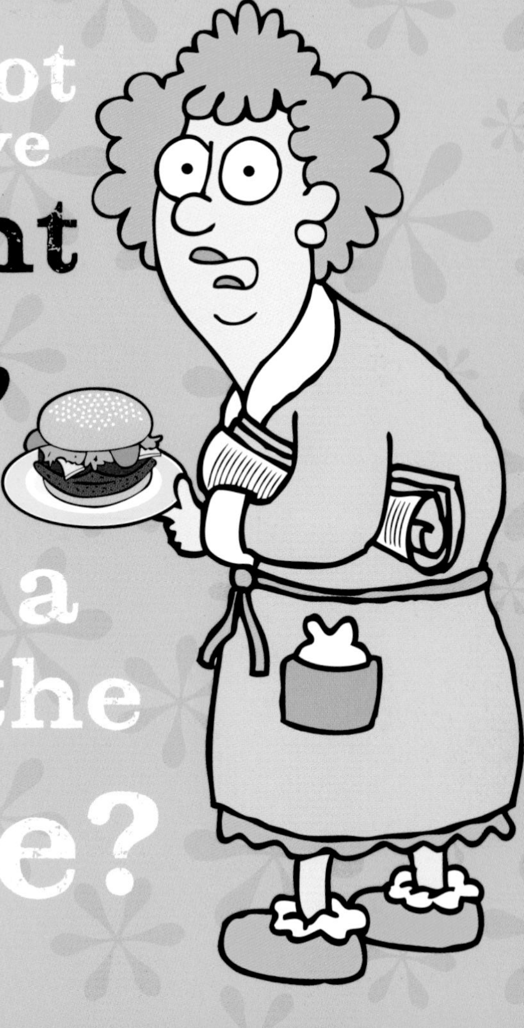

I don't like to think of myself as having an attitude problem.

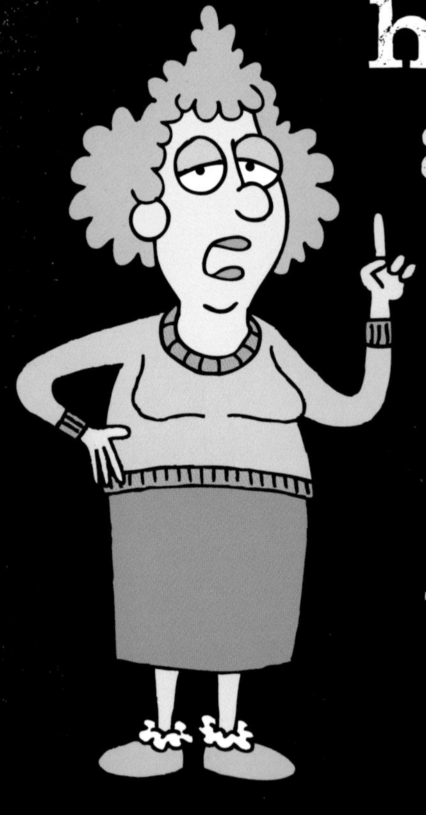

I like to think it's just I have a personality you can't handle.

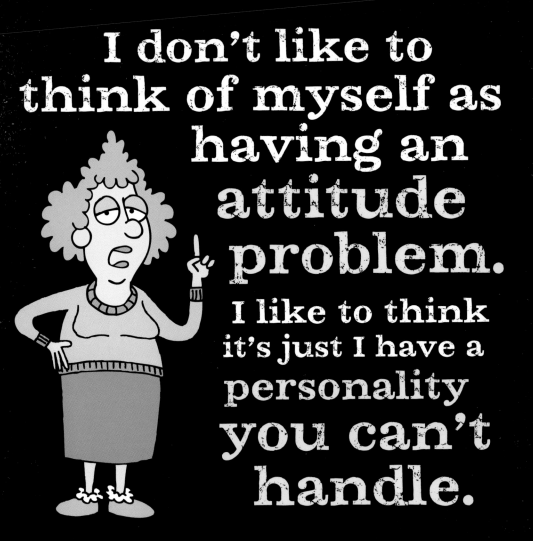

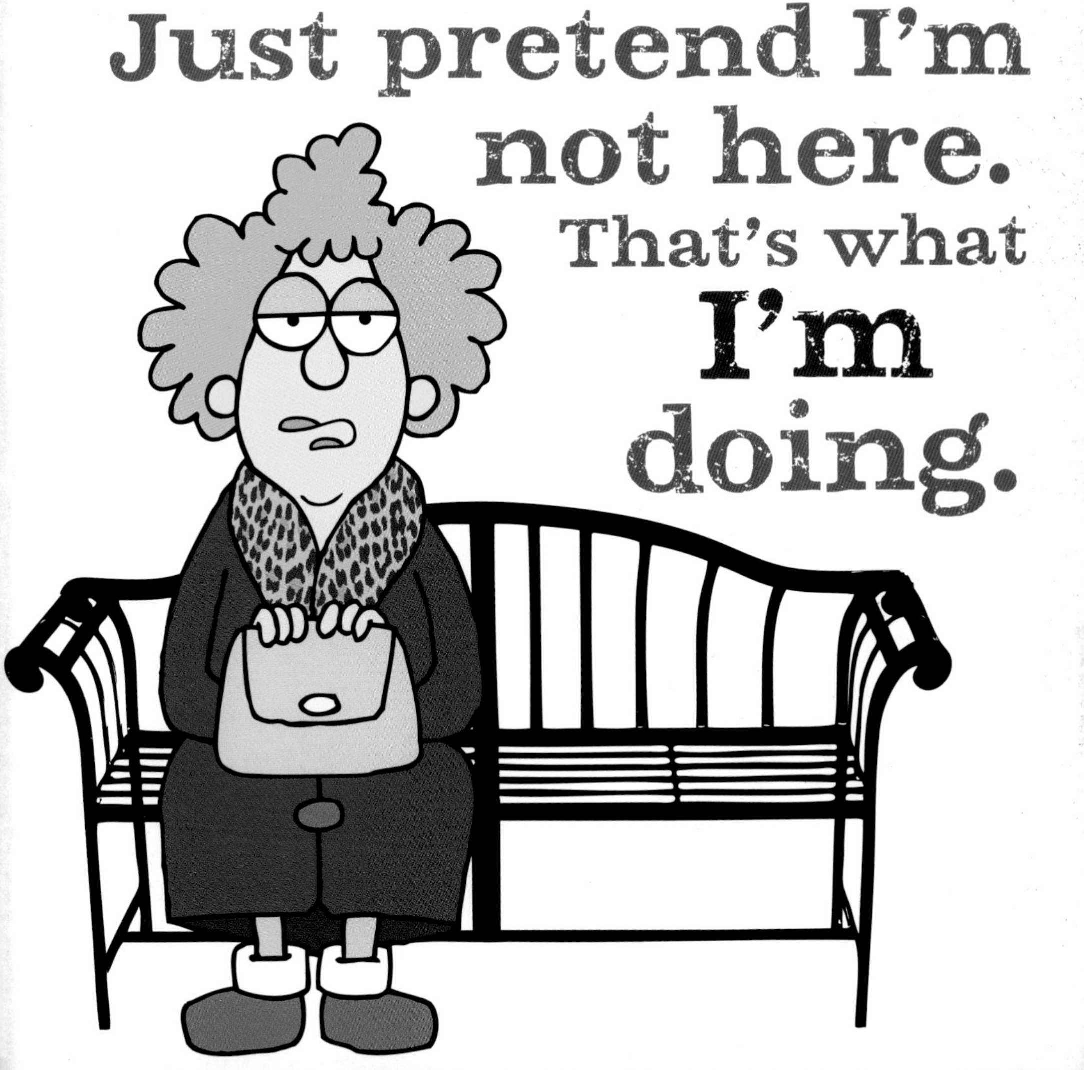
Just pretend I'm
not here.
That's what
I'm
doing.

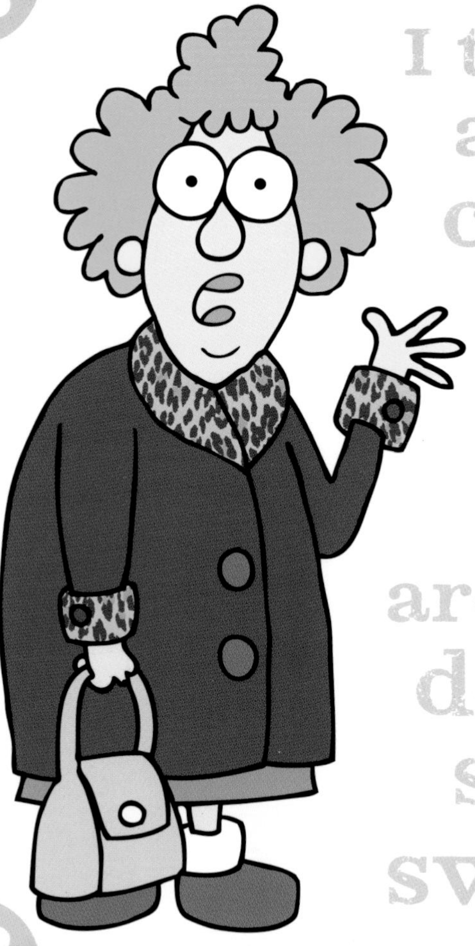

I think I'm allergic to chocolate. My ass and thighs are showing definite signs of swelling.

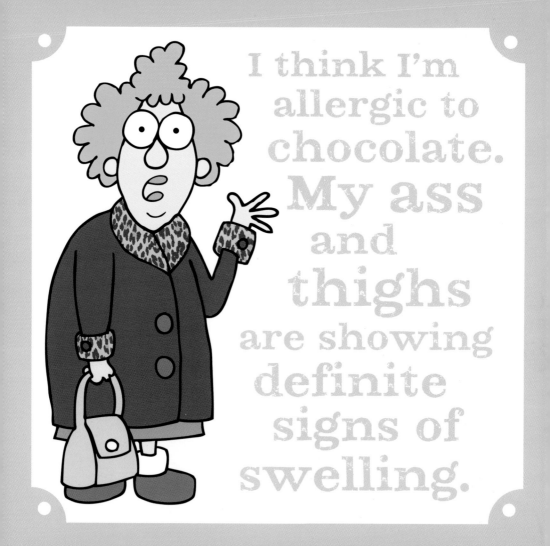

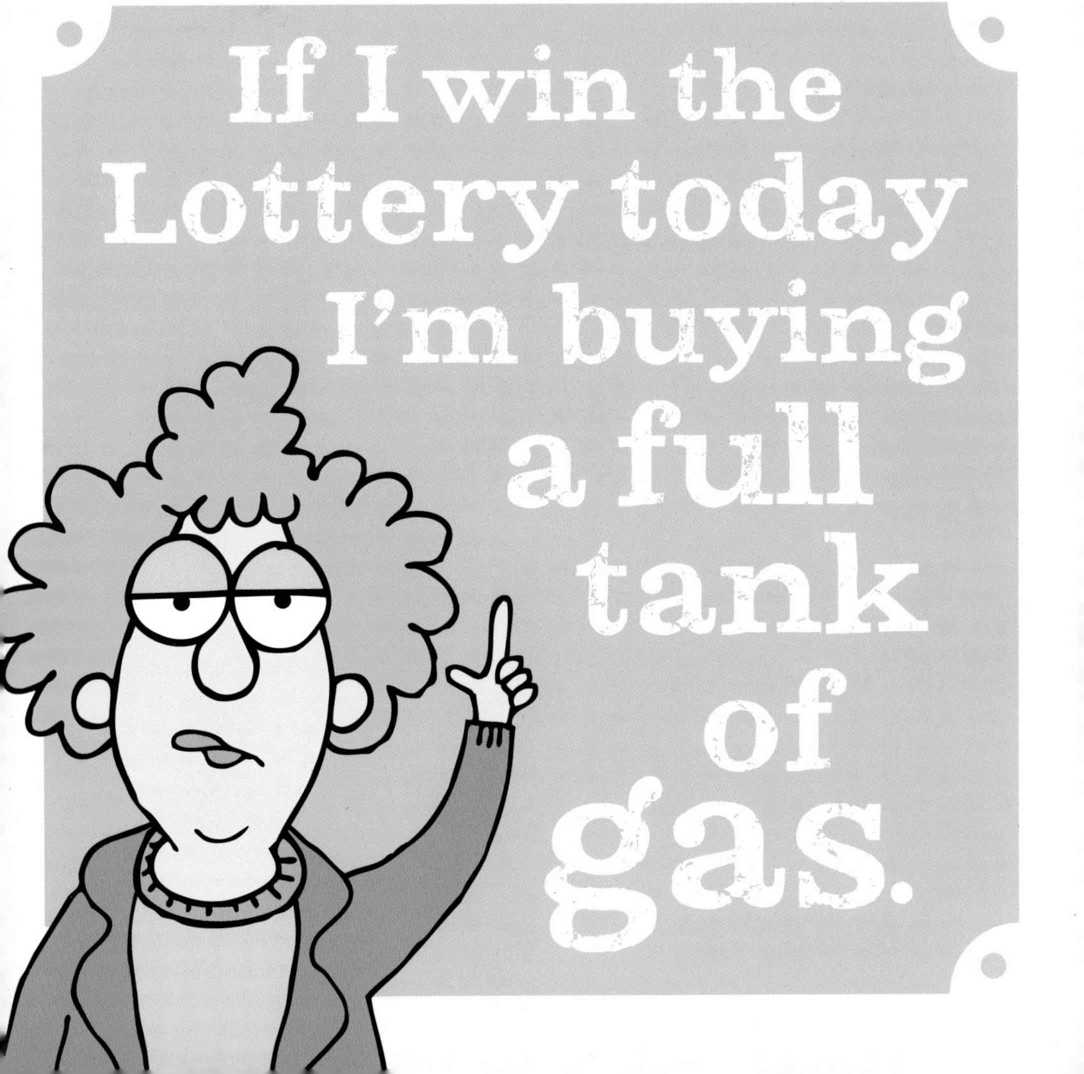
If I win the Lottery today I'm buying a full tank of gas.

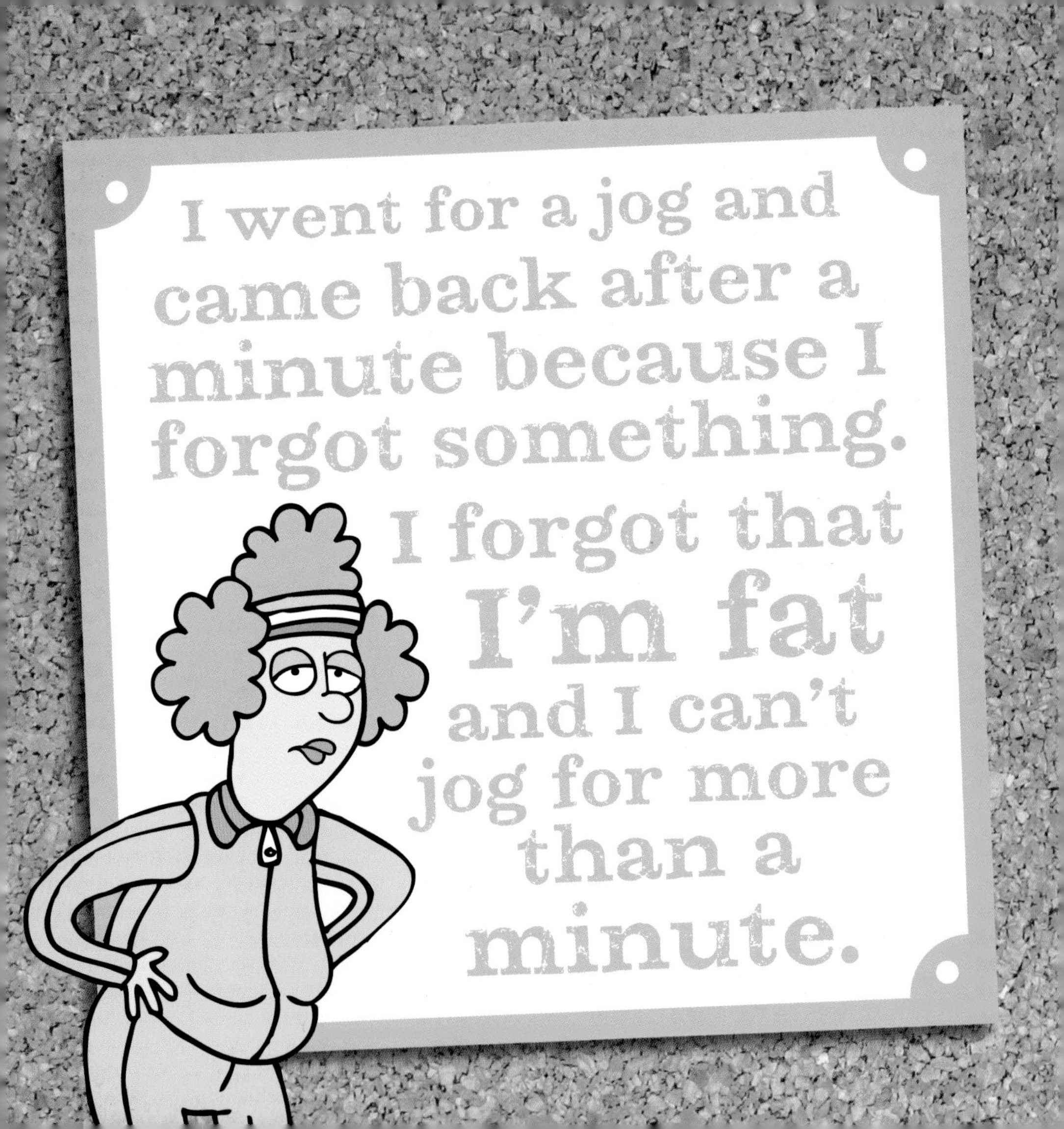
I went for a jog and came back after a minute because I forgot something.
I forgot that I'm fat and I can't jog for more than a minute.

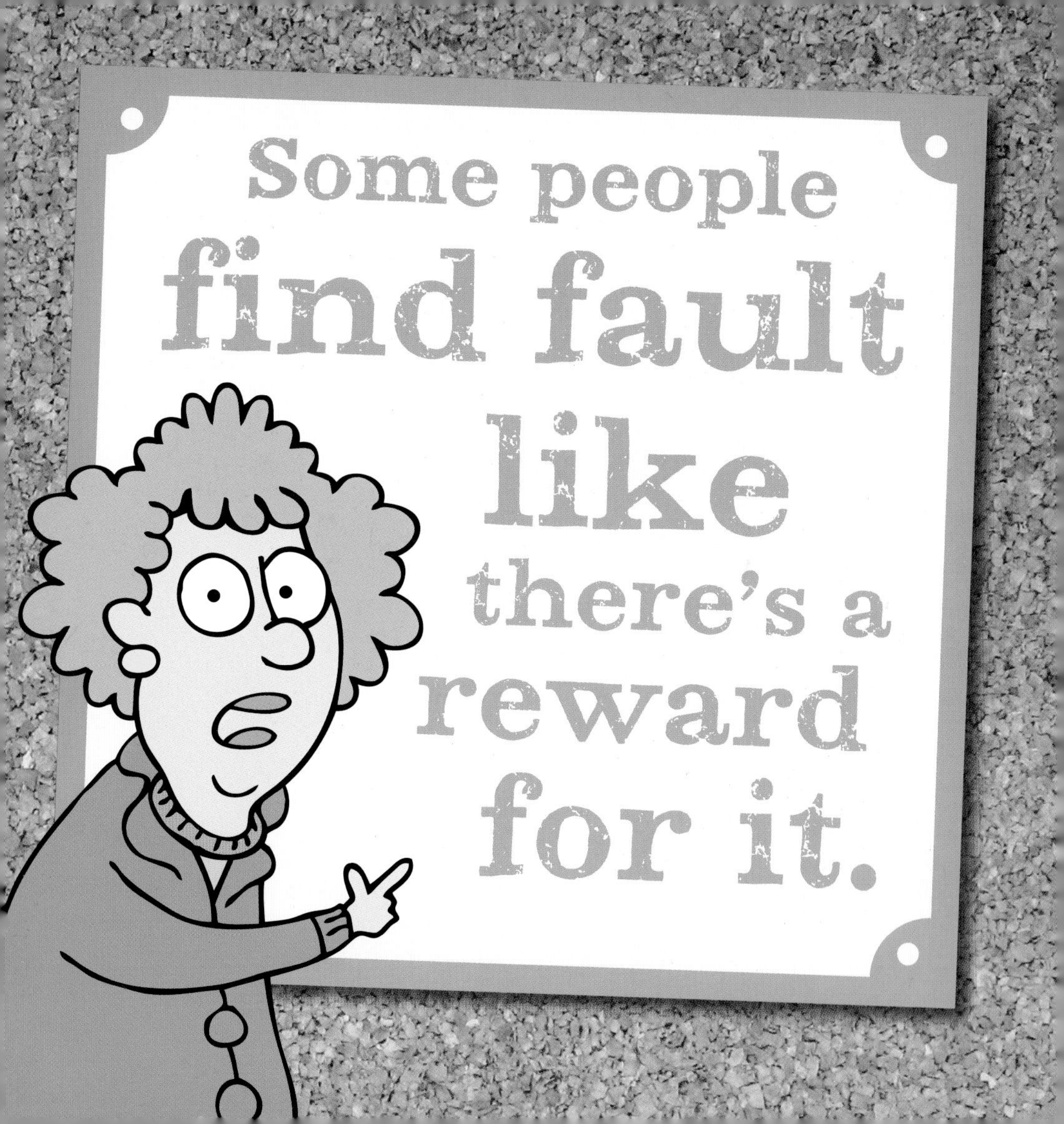
Some people find fault like there's a reward for it.

First Edition

17 16 15 14 13   5 4 3 2 1

Cartoons © 2013 Ced Backland

Published by
Gibbs Smith
P.O. Box 667
Layton, Utah 84041

1.800.835.4993 orders
www.gibbs-smith.com

Illustrations by Dave Iddon @
The Backland Studio
Interiors designed by Dave Iddon
Cover designed by Melissa Dymock
Printed and bound in China

Gibbs Smith books are printed on either recycled, 100% post-consumer
waste, FSC-certified papers or on paper produced from sustainable PEFC-
certified forest/controlled wood source. Learn more at www.pefc.org.

ISBN 13: 978-1-4236-3500-0